Lure of the Vampire:

A Pop Culture Reference Book

3rd Edition

By

Bertena Varney, M.A., M.Ed.

Plus, the Fiction Story: Lillian: A Vampire Story

by

Elizabeth Loraine and Bertena Varney

Indie Publishing House

GAINESVILLE, FL

Print Edition

Copyright © 2014 by Indie Publishing House
ISBN-10: 1500389803
ISBN-13: 978-1500389802

© Cover design by Paradox Book Cover Promotions – Patti
Roberts: http://paradoxbooktrailerproductions.blogspot.com.au/

Editing by BZHercules.com:
http://www.bzhercules.com/index.html

~~~DEDICATION PAGE~~~

This book is dedicated to my son, Tre' Varney, and my boyfriend, Samuel Hinds, as well as my students at Southcentral Community and Technical College. They have all really inspired me in different ways to finish this project!

And a special thanks to my research assistants and students, Kacie Henderson and Jeff Page. I would have never kept the anime, manga, and comic section straight if it wasn't for them!

And last but not least, to my dad and mom, who might not have understood everything I was doing, but were supportive nonetheless!

~~~TABLE OF CONTENTS~~~

~~~ABOUT THIS BOOK~~~

Lure of the Vampire was first published in June 2011 and is now being "revamped" to include more reviews, interviews, updated lists, and information.

Here is how the book is laid out:

Each of the chapters listed in the Table of Contents may contain one or more of the following:

- Lists of topics to help the reader find a quick list of information about that specific section.
- Links to websites with more specific information. These links have been chosen because they have been active for several years and are direct links to the topic at hand.
- Interviews of authors, actors, and real life vampires.
- Essays pertinent to each section.
- Excerpts of recent articles dealing with vampires in the news.
- Excerpts of reviews of books, movies, television shows, and more.

There is also an extensive bibliography at the end of the book. But, more importantly, we have added a free copy of the novella, *Lillian: A Vampire Story*. It is the wonderful beginning of a fiction story written by Elizabeth Loraine based upon my role-playing character, Lillian. It is included at the end of this book for your enjoyment.

This is a perfect book for those vampire fans that want more information about all aspects of the vampire, not just mythology or pop culture, but a well-rounded touch on all things related to the vampire. The websites listed are perfect for finding more information and the fast facts are great for a fast reference. *Lure* gives you a taste of the vampire that hopefully will have you craving more information about this misunderstood creature.

So, pick a chapter and enjoy your journey into the dark world of the vampire.

~~~ACKNOWLEDGEMENTS~~~

Thanks to everyone who helped me research and create the first, second, and the final editions of this book, especially my Southcentral Community and Technical College students that volunteered as my research assistants - Jeff Page and Kacie Henderson. They really helped me when it came to the anime, manga, and comic section. Without them, I would still be up to my neck in the multiple vampire resources. Thank you a lot!

Thanks to the vampire fans that bought my book and, in return, helped me with suggestions and new links to add to this edition.

Thanks to all of my friends who have been very supportive in this endeavor. I could not have succeeded without any of you.

Thanks to my students who inspire me to keep learning, just as much as I try to do the same for them. I really do learn something new in our classroom each semester. They do keep me striving to learn more so that I can become a better teacher for them. Remember, never put yourself in a box and always be who you want to be, not what others want you to be. Life is much more enjoyable if you do.

~~~PREFACE TO THE LURE OF THE VAMPIRE ~~~

The Lure of the Vampire began as research for my master's thesis, *The Search for the Lure of the Vampire.* I was a lifelong student and was completing my Masters in Social Science and Education when I found that I needed one more class in order to graduate with my degree. This would not be a problem for most students, but I had already completed all the sociology and history classes that my college offered while completing my undergraduate Social Science Education degree and my Sociology and Criminology Masters. So, I was at a loss.

At that time, I was teaching part time as an adjunct at Eastern Kentucky University. One day, I was speaking with a colleague. She asked me about my problem and what I needed to do to complete the program. I told her the details and she said that her sister taught at my alma mater, Morehead State University. I contacted her sister and, after explaining my predicament to her, was very pleased when she agreed to let me build my own course of independent study.

She asked me what interested me. I told her that I had always taken the opportunity to steer any of my extra papers or studies towards the subject of vampires, citing the paper I did in history class on the history of the monster and for criminology, where I studied the subculture of modern vampires. She looked at me, interested but skeptical. We discussed the fact that pop culture has become very popular among the academic realm and, as such, had been deemed a legitimate study. She then agreed that if I could provide academic research and several other resources, then she would allow me to use this as my final class.

Well, she approved the study and I was off on what would become the most exciting semester of my life. I finally was allowed to read all the books, watch all the movies, and research all the blogs and websites about vampires that I wanted to, but for a valid academic purpose. But, a semester was not enough to time to research my paper because there is no one specific place, no definitive websites that are available for anyone wanting information about vampires. There are sites available, but it takes time to find them and, many times, they are outdated or abandoned. As a result, I decided that I was going to continue my research and develop a reference tool that would help others like me who are researching and writing about vampires – whether academically, as fans, or as fiction authors.

It was a very slow process at first. I researched and compiled information, but it wasn't until January 2010 when I became unemployed that I decided to dedicate all of my time to writing this book. I found a new avenue of research through Examiner.com, where I was given the columns for the Vampire Examiner and the True Blood Examiner. This allowed me national exposure to vampire fans and authors, many of whom have helped me through this process whether by providing links to websites, proofreading the manuscript, contributing articles, or just standing by me when I felt overwhelmed and overly anxious about this project.

After the first edition came out in June 2011, I could not stop researching and finding more resources about the sexy creature of the night. So, after compiling this research, I have added it to the first edition and hope that my thirst for the bloodsucker has paid off and provided you, the reader, with some special editions to this reference book.

Each year, the vampire continues to seduce those who love his history and literature, so this is never a finished project, but a never-ending endeavor.

However, for today, the third and final edition of this book is now ready for you, the reader, to use for your own research into this night creature known as the vampire. I hope that you find this book as much of a resource as I have. There are lists, websites, interviews, and very telling essays about vampires. The book begins with the history and mythology of the vampire and continues through literature, television, movies, games, modern vampires, and much more. This book has been an adventure in itself.......

Please enjoy YOUR study of the creature of the night.

> "Whether we read books and watch films about vampires for psychological reasons or simply for entertainment purposes, each of us keeps the vampire myth alive. While we may be able to understand rationally that vampires do not exist, who among us does not start at the shadow at the window or the squeak in the dark?"
>
> ~Daniel C. Scarvone, author of *Vampires*

~~~INTRODUCTION~~~

The Lure of the Vampire is a pop culture reference book for writers, vampire fans, students, and teachers who love to study the mysterious creature of the night. This book is for the fanatics who sit up at night and watch reruns of *Buffy* for the hundredth time, the Twi-hards that line up for hours before the show just to glimpse the newest *Twilight* movie, the Truebies who all knows that "waiting sucks" between each season of *True Blood,* and for those diehard traditionalists that balk at all of this "new" vampire craze.

The Lure of the Vampire is also for the new writers who love creating their own worlds where the vampires may be aristocratic and romantic or dark and dangerous; the world where there are castles, heaving bosoms, chivalry, and danger of loving a vampire, the dreams of so many women in today's world.

And finally, *The Lure of the Vampire* is a book for those who love to study all aspects of the vampire in both pop culture and the world. Whether they are the historian who loves tracing the evolution of the vampire or the sociologist who wants to explore the world of those that live the lifestyle, readers will find resources here to help them in their quest for knowledge of this lifestyle.

The Lure of the Vampire is divided into ten sections, beginning with mythology and ending with modern vampires. Within each section, there are lists that will help the reader learn basic and fun facts about that section's topic. Links to websites are

provided to ensure that the reader may find more information about that section without having to search for it on the Internet or in other books. To help supplement a particular subject within that topic, there are personal essays or interviews that give the reader a personal look from the author's perspective. For example, *Lure of the Dead Boyfriend* provides the reader with a look at why women love vampire romance while exploring the vampire as a soul mate, an erotic lover, and an escape from the real world.

Lure of the Vampire provides unique interviews with vampire authors, role players, and those that live the lifestyle. The reader can delve into the world of a creator of an alternate reality or learn more about those whose lives lead them to embrace vampirism as a way of life.

Lure of the Vampire is a complete pop culture reference book for those who enjoy vampires and their impact on society. It provides an extensive bibliography that will allow the reader the opportunity for additional independent study.

~~~ ARE VAMPIRES GOING BACK INTO THE COFFIN?~~~

As I begin this third and final edition of *Lure of the Vampire,* I think back to 2008 when I began this journey and how popular vampires were during that time. You could not turn on the television without an advertisement for a television show or a new movie that had a unique story of the vampire and how they are trying to survive either in modern or Victorian society. From the teen *Twilight* movies, *True Blood* television show, or the *Scooby Doo* cartoons that have Scooby and Shaggy running from the vampire, everywhere you turned, there were vampires. Vampire-related items were abundant as well – vampire slaying kits, fangmakers, and toys for kids.

It seemed that the vampire craze of the 1980s was back. Those of us that grew up with *The Lost Boys, Fright Night,* and *My Best Friend is a Vampire* became super excited that this wonderful, scary, and, at times, sexy monster was back. Yes, many of us hated the idea of the sparkling and whining *Twilight* vampires, but in hindsight, we have to give credit to the teens and their love of this modern vampire as the reason why we got to enjoy the revival of the vampire.

This excitement over the new vampire craze allowed us to enjoy books by authors such as Charlaine Harris, Molly Harper, Melissa de la Cruz, Elizabeth Loraine, Joann I. Martin Sowles, and Lynda Hilburn. It opened up vampires to a new reader. Even though the depiction of the vampire did become romanticized in many ways, most of these authors tried to show the true monster of the vampire while staying true to the mythology and stories that we came to love reading. But, Mrs. Harris, Mrs. Harper, and Mrs. Dela Cruz ended their popular series because the story had been told and it was time to try other projects, leaving fans waiting for their next series dealing with witches, psychics, and other supernatural creatures.

This new craze brought about television shows such as *True Blood, Vampire Diaries, Blood Ties, Being Human,* and recently, *Dracula* and *The Originals.* Each of these shows offered various types of vampires, what I call both fanged and defanged, those that embrace being a vampire and hate their true nature. We were introduced to Eric, Klaus, Damon, Mitchell, Aiden, Henry, Bill, and Stefan as well as strong female vampires such as Caroline, Rebekkah, Katherine, Pam, and Jessica. But, many of these have or are ended. *BBC Being Human* and *Blood Ties* have ended, *True Blood* will be over this summer, and *Dracula* has been cancelled after one season. This just leaves *The Vampire Diaries* and *The Originals* to hold the vampire television shows alive for fans.

There are two new cable shows called *Strain* on FX and *Dusk til Dawn* coming to El- Rey, but most fans are really not putting much hope on these shows when zombies and witches seem to be taking the vampires' place on television.

However, the movies were what really brought the craze back to the vampire fans. *Dark Shadows, Fright Night, Daybreakers, Thirst, Vamp, Abraham Lincoln Vampire Hunter, Hotel Transylvania, Priest, Underworld, the Blade Trilogies,* and *Dylan Dog* were just a few of the many vampire movies that were flooding the theater. It seemed like every time you turned on the television, there was an advertisement for another vampire movie.

But, last year, the vampire movies were lacking. *Phobia, Vamp, Fright Night 2,* and *Byzantium* basically went straight to DVD or had limited theater showings. And *Vampire Academy* made a weak showing at the theater, not being the hit that the author and fans had expected.

So, yes, there are a few strong television shows like *The Vampire Diaries* and *The Originals,* and a few authors that are still writing about vampires. But, as I predict, many of them will take their books that hold supernatural creatures and begin to market them more as supernatural and not vampire in order to continue their series.

So, it is sad for me to say, but I think that the vampires are going back into the coffin for another decade or so. Yes, there are diehard fans that will always love the mythology of vampires and re-watch every movie ever made, but for the general population, it looks like vampires have lost their sparkle and/or fright appeal as before.

But, the good news is, that since they hit the books in the 1850s and the movie screen in the 1920s, they will return stronger and different each time. The most exciting part is to see what the future talented authors and screenwriters will have in store for us this next time they make their appearance in pop culture. Vampires are immortal creatures both in fiction and mythology and, because of this, they will return! But, when and as what is left to be seen.

So, goodbye for now, you royal and frightful creature, and know that I will be here waiting for your next return!

~~~VAMPIRES IN MYTHOLOGY~~~

Since the beginning of time, there have been stories of the great creature of the night. Vampires and vampire-like creatures have been described in every society as either a way to explain death, an angry god, or simply to entertain. Vampires are not the new craze of today, but the creature that has survived throughout time.

There are always debates as to whether Lilith is a vampire, a succubus, or a demon, and if some of the "myths" only apply to vampires or should include the fact that many of the people who believed vampires, witches, ghosts, and werewolves were real in their world and used many of the "safeguards" and superstitions to cover all of these creatures. What I have done is chosen those that I have seen referred to more than others; ones that have been used in the media, and ones that have been agreed upon by most vampirologists such as myself. This is by no means a complete list of the types of vampires that have been talked about and feared throughout mythology, but it is a list that writers or fans can begin with and then later explore more of what they are specifically looking for.

In this section, you will find lists ranging from origins of the word "vampire" to tips on how to protect yourself, as well as a very thorough essay on *Vampires as Religious Icons*.

I have also added shorts that tell specifically about vampires in mythology.

So, enjoy your trip back in time as you learn how this beautiful yet monstrous creature came to be.

~~10 Origins of the Word "Vampire"~~

- Greek – *vrykolakas*
- Romanian – *strigoli*
- German - *Vampir*
- Bulgarian – *vampire*
- Croatian - *upir/upirina*
- Czech and Slovak - *upír*
- Ukrainian - *upyr*
- Russian - *upyr'*
- Old East Slavic - *upir'*
- French – *vampyre*

~~10 Ways to Protect Yourself from a Vampire~~

- Hang garlic around your neck as well as around the entrance to your house.
- Use religious symbols, such as Crucifixes, Holy Water, and Rosaries, on yourself and in your home.
- Sprinkle mustard seed around a vampire to repel the creature and also to distract him because of his compulsive need to count the seeds.
- Remain on consecrated ground like a church or cemetery.
- Escape across running water.
- Never invite one into your home and, if you have, revoke the invitation quickly.
- Hang or carry mirrors to repel them.

- Surround your home with thorny roses to ensure they get tangled up and cannot escape or move.
- Use weapons such as guns with silver bullets, blow torches, and axes to decapitate.
- Grab your trusty stake and think "What would Buffy do?"

~~10 Ways to Become a Vampire after Death~~

- Any dead body that is jumped over by a cat or dog.
- A wounded body that has not been cleansed.
- A witch that rebelled against the Roman Catholic Church when they were alive is rumored to become a vampire.
- Anyone who commits suicide will return to life as a vampire.
- Possession by a demon will result in returning as a vampire.
- Vampires are fallen angels that are sent here to continue living as the undead until they right what they did wrong.
- Bitten by another vampire.
- A vampire shares his blood with a human.
- Born a *dhampir* or half human and half vampire.
- Be a revenant of an evil human or demon, depending upon the culture.

~~10 Ways to Not Become a Vampire after Death~~

- When a person dies, the family should stop the hands on the clock because they believe that it will stop time and that this will preserve the dead person's soul until they could be buried on consecrated or holy ground.

- Be baptized at birth and be buried upside down in consecrated ground.
- Cover mirrors in your home when people die. This will keep the mirrors from taking the dead person's soul and leaving them a vampire. This was also done in some homes as a rule, even if the person was still alive. Once you finish with the mirror, you cover it so that it cannot steal your soul, thus turning you into a vampire instantly.
- Be buried with garlic and iron.
- Place scythes near the grave to keep demons from possessing your body.
- Stake the body to the ground in the grave.
- Cut off the head of the corpse at burial.
- Burn the corpse.
- Be entombed by a witch.
- Drain the body of blood.

~~10 Powers that Vampires Possess~~

- Hypnosis, mind control, or compelling their victim.
- Flying, scaling walls, and super-fast speed.
- Shape-shifting into wolves, bats, fog, rats, fleas, birds, frogs, insects, and numerous other creatures.
- Super strength ranging from super human to the Superman type strength.
- The ability to control nature, including animals and weather.
- Improved senses such as night vision, super hearing, smell for tracking, etc.

- Reading minds, smoothing emotions, and seeing the future.
- Fast-healing ability ranging from immediate to slow healing after feeding.
- Creation of other vampires for love, companionship, or even massive armies to take over the world.
- And, of course, immortality and youthful beauty.

~~10 Signs of a Being a Vampire~~

- An infant that is born with hair on the back of its hand.
- Anyone born a redhead or who is a "ginger."
- Mother committed suicide while pregnant.
- Mother ate or drank something "unclean."
- Sensitive to light.
- Someone who is anemic or craves blood.
- A baby born with a caul or born with a birth defect.
- Anyone with obsessive compulsive disorder, hence the belief that vampire have to stop and count anything that is dropped in front of them.
- One who was born the 7th son of the 7th son.
- If you were born with blue eyes, you may be a vampire.

~~10 Signs that You are Dealing with a Vampire~~

- They have no reflection in a mirror or a shiny surface.
- They only come out in the night. This is not because they will "explode" or "turn to dust"; this isn't always true. Dracula was out in the day, but his powers are greatly diminished in the day time.
- They won't enter a home without being invited.

- Religious symbols frighten them. The symbol depends upon the religion or the lack thereof the religion of the said vampire.
- Hypnotic, glowing eyes that range from red to golden.
- Never eats in front of you.
- Has foul breath and is repelled by garlic.
- Has pale skin and sometimes long nails or pointy ears.
- They cast no shadow.
- Is unusually aristocratic, rich, and influential in the area, especially if they just moved to town.

~~10 Vampires in Mythology~~

- *Kukudhi* can be found in Albania. This vampire was said to be created from people who were guilty of unspeakable crimes in their lives and were never caught or punished. Upon their deaths, they would become vampires that spread this evil and infection all around the world.
- The Alps were Austrian vampires who could shape shift into anything and would visit women in their sleep. They would not only drink the blood of humans, but also eat them.
- The Cherokee believe that any witch who eats her husband's liver will become an Ojibwa or vampire.
- An *Aswang* is a Filipino female vampire that was beautiful by day and a monster at night who used her tongue to suck the blood from her victims.
- The *Penanggalan* or "Penny," as she has been nicknamed, is the Malaysian vampire that would disembowel herself at night and fly through the skies.

As she would fly, she would sparkle in the moonlight, thus attracting her victims to her.

- The Chinese *Chiang Shih* is a zombie-like ghost that would seek out the souls of the dead, especially before that soul left the dead's body. These monsters were blind and used their other senses to survive. Instead of sucking blood, they would suck the breath out of their victims.
- The vampire in Ghana is called the *Adze* and is a ghost-like vampire that preys on children.
- The African witch what leaves her body at night and searches for babies to eat is called the *Obayifo*.
- The *Feu-follet* is a local vampire in African-American folklore. They believed that the soul could return to earth and drink blood from others, so they would sit up for three nights to be prepared to smite down the body if it would rise from the grave. This is one idea of where the tradition originated that many southern families sit up with the bodies for three days and nights. The other is in respect to the time that Jesus was out of the grave after the crucifixion.
- The *Afrit* is the Arabian vampiric smoke-like spirit who was murdered and exacts revenge on its murderer. It is said that you can put a nail through the blood spill and hold the spirit in the earth. The television show, *True Blood*, used the idea of an "*Ifrit*," which is simply a smoke demon who does the same as the above *Afrit* on their vampire television show.

~~3 Types of Vampires in Mythology~~

- Non corporeal vampires fly, float, and disappear like a ghost.
- Revenant vampires are zombie-like with no personality.

- Personality vampires have a personality and are like the humans that they once were.

~~Did You Know?~~

- Many people believe that vampires are obsessive compulsive and that if you drop seeds or millet in front of them, then they have to stop and pick it up. They can only follow you if or when all of the seeds are counted. This is called "apotropaic" and is the basis for the idea of *Sesame Street*'s Count von Count.
- Another example of apotropaic is for the homeowner to lay an animal head at your door. The vampire can't go anywhere until they have counted every hair on the animal. This is said to be true for knots as well.
- In Christian beliefs, the Crucifix and stake must be made from the aspen tree, the tree that was used to sacrifice Jesus. There is also the belief that silver is bad for vampires because Judas betrayed Jesus for thirty pieces of silver. But, the story of Judas does not stop there; the idea of obsessive counting was also adopted by the Christians. They believed that Judas's greed was passed on to his children, thus the need to count coins if they are tossed at their feet.
- The Blackthorn shrub was also supposed to be good protection. It was the thorny shrub that was used to make Jesus's crown at his crucifixion.
- The Greeks believed that the color blue protected them from vampires.
- If you place coins on the eyes of the dead to pay their way into the underworld, their soul is safe and they will not return as a vampire.

- A *Dhamphir* or *Dhampyre* is usually a daywalker whose father is a vampire and mother is a human. Many times, the situation that resulted in pregnancy was very violent in nature. They are usually not vampires, but often take the role of a vampire hunter to seek revenge. Examples of dhamphirs are Blade, Rayne, and even Renesmee from *Twilight*, even though her situation does not fit the typical dhamphir model.
- Don Augustin Calmet published several reports on vampires in Hungary and Moravia that led everyone to believe that vampires were real in the mid-1800s.
- *Chupacabra* or goat sucker is an animal that is said to have been seen throughout Latin America, Mexico, and the Southwestern part of the US. It is said to attack animals and drain them of their blood. It is said that when seen, it is as big as a dog. There is no proof of this animal.
- Many people believe that if you are unfortunately bitten by a vampire, then they should find that vampire, burn them, and drink the ashes
- To protect you from a vampire attack, simply eat bread made from the blood of a vampire.

~Why were Women Created as Vampires in Mythology?~

While doing research for this chapter, I found that many of the first vampires in mythology were women. The second interesting fact that I noticed was that many female vampires' fates centered on pregnancy and childbirth. It would appear that these women were cursed simply for being female. For example, many would die during childbirth because of something that could only be blamed on the female, thus becoming a seductress monster of the night. But, the fear and distrust of women did not stop there. The stories would continue to evolve into an even more gruesome monster by turning these women into baby killers that would be feared by families. It appears that many times women were used as the bad creatures to explain things that they did not understand back then, such as sudden infant death syndrome, miscarriages, adulterous behavior, and more.

The stories began with Lilith and the idea that she was the first wife of Adam in Hebrew mythology. She would not be submissive to Adam during sex and was exiled from Eden. In some stories, she became a vampire-like demon and, in other stories, she began procreating with demons and populated the earth with evil spawn at a rate of thousands. The story then goes on to say that God was not happy with this and sent his angels to destroy her children and to demand that she stop. She then in turn killed the human children of God. Many Hebrew women would tie talismans that would deter Lilith. This was their protection of what they did not understand was sudden infant death syndrome or "crib death."

Greek mythology has Lamia, the secret lover of Zeus, who, like many other of his lovers, was found out by his wife Hera. Out of vengeance, Hera killed all of Lamia's babies and, in response, Lamia attacked the children of the followers of Hera. Her sucking of the children's blood is what gained her the name of a vampire. This again is the explanation of babies and children dying from fevers and in their sleep.

In Malaysia, Pennangallan, or Penny, as she is known by many, is another female vampire to which the death of children is attributed. Penny would detach her fanged body and fly around with her disemboweled body glistening in the moonlight. She would search for pregnant women to drink from, thus explaining miscarriages or still born deaths.

So, as you can see from the above examples, many times, the female vampires were used to explain "female issues" that in many cultures were taboo or not discussed in the presence of men. There was also the lack of medical advances that would explain the deaths of children and pregnant mothers. Thus, the duality of the good and bad impression of the roles of women in regards to motherhood in society.

~Vampires and Religion: Vampires used as Religious Icons~

Introduction

The images of demons that drain humans of their blood and roam the earth as damned creatures reinforces the Christian idea that vampires are unholy creatures that need blood to survive. This drinking of human blood is forbidden in the Old Testament, where it is actually set out as a "sin."

But popular culture's need to create fiction using religious icons and events has become increasingly popular within the last decade. The identification of oneself in these stories shows that the vampire is not simply an evil revenant, but a device of society to help one seek to fulfill a void in one's life. The lust of empowerment, the need for acceptance, the search for redemption, and the question of eternal life has been the lure that the vampire has over today's society.

The Story of Lilith and the Search for Empowerment

Lilith is the mythological first wife of Adam. According to Hebrew mythology, she was created first, but refused to be submissive to Adam, especially during sex. She did not want to lie beneath or to be submissive to a man, thus she was banished from the Garden of Eden.

From this point on in mythology, there are varying stories that range from Lilith becoming a demon, to her living her life as a vampire. She has been credited with killing newborn babies, men, and the massacre of millions. The stories exist in almost every culture whether she is a vampire, a demon, or just an evil creature of the night. She is also represented by the night owl, screech owl, and a blue-like demon.

Lilith is always associated with the power of seduction. She is said to have had sex with demons and populated the earth with her demon children. As a result, God sent angels to kill this multitude of children at a rate of 100 per day. This angered Lilith and she began to kill human babies, thus her reputation as a baby killer.

She has been credited with being the Queen of Sheba as well as numerous other creatures in countless other cultures such as Babylonia, England, Greece. Each mythological persona became a true icon of female strength and sacrifice that evolved into legends of her being a demon and succubus.

She has even been credited for being the beginning of the vampire bloodlines. This story was used in the creation of her character in the *World of Darkness* role-playing game, "Vampire the Masquerade." More of her role as a vampire can be found under Cain in this section of the essay.

But, Lilith's choice for independence over male companionship has been a theme that has survived until modern times. Today, she has been reborn into many forms that have retold her story. She has been the daughter of Dracula in Marvel Comics and an ancient demon in the SyFy original movie, *Darklight*. Lilith's story in each evolved into female characters that were created by the male counterpart and, while evil in nature, in each role, she became the most powerful creature in the story. She overcame the negative male belief and took up the fight for empowerment for females.

Focusing more on her iconic image of female empowerment, Lilith was chosen as the symbol to represent female musicians in their fight to gain equal treatment in the male-dominated radio industry. The Lilith Fair, a Woodstock-type event, was created to draw attention to the fact that radio DJs were giving more air time to male performers. The fair was successful in allowing new and popular female musicians to share the radio airwaves equally with men, as well as allowing new artists to break into the business.

Lilith might have begun as a night creature with wings and talons that drank babies' blood, but today, she is seen as a symbol of woman's refusal to be submissive to man, not just intimately, but in all walks of life. She gives strength to the women in society to choose independence and free thinking over doing what one is told they should do. Her popularity in today's society is shown by the increase of her character being reborn and changed in modern science fiction. Each time her story is told, she allows society to see her not just as the angry female who is vengeful but, as shown in *Darklight,* the strong female who has the power to seek empowerment over her past and to lead her male counterparts to the destruction of evil in their world. Lilith has fortified her role as the icon of female empowerment for today's society.

The Story of Cain and the Search for Acceptance

In modern society as well as the Judeo-Christian churches and synagogues, Cain's story is one that is more familiar than Lilith's. Cain was the first son to be born of Adam and Eve and expected to be the continuation of the family line, the line that was to lead to King David and eventually to the birth of Jesus Christ. In this society, being the first born son was held in the highest regard, as it was with Cain.

Cain was the overseer and protector of the fruits and vegetables of the earth and his youngest brother, Abel, was the overseer of the animals of the earth. Each brother was expected to give freely of their offering to Yahweh or God. One day, Cain was to make their offering to Yahweh. Abel gave his best and Cain gave his second best. As a result, the sacrifice was not accepted. This shamed him and his family. In a fit of rage, Cain spilled the first drop of blood upon the pure earth by striking his brother down.

As a punishment, Yahweh cast Cain from his promised land and into the darkness. It is written that there was a mark put upon him that would protect him from being harmed by the others that lived in the dark land. Many people translate that into a curse, while others believe that it gave him strength, but would isolate him from man. All the Bible says is that Cain left and wandered upon the earth and searched for acceptance from others.

What happened to Cain in the darkness is where pop culture has taken liberty with the story. Cain's largest role in pop culture has been in White Wolf's role-playing game *Vampire: The Masquerade*. Within this game's story, Cain is wandering in eternal damnation upon the earth. One night, he comes across Lilith, whom we spoke of in the preceding section. Lilith is a very beautiful and seductive lady. She talks him into embracing his curse by sharing her life essence or blood with him, thus releasing his power from within. By exchanging blood with Cain, he becomes her son in blood and this exchange brings forth his power over darkness.

As the story goes on, he wanders the darkness alone and he strengthens his power. But, because he is alone, he becomes lonely and decides that he wants to share his power, even though Lilith warns him not to. He comes upon a city and he shares his power with three gentlemen who become known as the second generation. They are now his children who love him unconditionally, or so he thinks.

Because he is no longer alone, Cain finally finds happiness through acceptance and friendship with these men. He makes it unlawful for them to share their gift with anyone, but these men become greedy and want more power. So, they choose to share this power with hundreds more, thus ignoring their sire's decree. The children of the second generation are not as loyal to the teachings of Cain and create yet a fourth and unruly animalistic generation.

This fourth generation is so greedy for power that they turn on their sires and kill them. In the story book of the White Wolf game, this is when Yahweh causes the great flood to come forth and to destroy the chaos that is on His earth, thus causing the destruction of the world. In the end, Cain is once again alone and left to wander the earth, thus gaining the nickname of the Wandering Jew.

Cain's stories have been told and retold through each character's creation in groups playing *Vampire: The Masquerade*. The story of his search for acceptance has shown resilience, even through the real-life, news-making scandal of the young vampire from Kentucky, Rod Ferrell.

When news hit that he and his vampire clan had killed his girlfriend's parents because he wanted to advance through the vampire ranks and to have a higher level of acceptance in the vampiric world, the world was shocked. According to Court TV, Ferrell and his clan of vampire followers brutalized the

Wendorfs and, as a seal of their deed, they proceeded to drink the couple's blood.

In court, Ferrell stated that his idea of a vampire clan came from the White Wolf game, *Vampire the Masquerade*. He had an obsession with the game and found acceptance with other area outcasts whom he would later label as his clan. White Wolf was found not to be responsible for Ferrell's action.

But this violence is only a dark blemish on the shadow of Cain's use as an icon for society's search for acceptance in both the physical and spiritual world. In legend and in the game, the crimson-headed Cain can be seen wandering the earth, sometimes alone or with another red-haired demon rumored to be Lilith.

The Story of Judas and the Search for Redemption

Another wandering Jew that is referred to as a vampire is a third crimson-haired icon named Judas Iscariot. Judas was a disciple of Christ and the one responsible for His arrest by Pontius Pilate's guards. He betrayed Christ by a single kiss on the cheek, for which his reward was thirty pieces of silver. He later regretted the action and threw the silver coins into the temple and went off to hang himself.

Judas's story as a vampire begins with his hanging. In vampire lore, anyone who commits suicide becomes a vampire because the soul is not allowed to enter heaven. That, combined with the fact that Judas had red hair (which was another sign of vampirism), sealed him as the most popular of all the religious icons that are portrayed as a vampire in pop culture. According to the movie *Dracula 2000,* Judas is the Dracula that we have come to know throughout history.

33

Dracula 2000 begins in present day with Van Helsing guarding the drained body of Dracula, until he can finally find a way to kill the evil creature. In order to stay alive, Van Helsing injects Dracula's blood into himself to maintain immortality.

Van Helsing is married. His wife becomes pregnant and bears a child with the blood of Dracula in her veins. Dracula awakens and searches for this child named Lucy. He finally captures her and is on the rooftop, discussing why he is so angry with God. At that time, he reveals that he is actually Judas Iscariot, the disciple and betrayer of Jesus Christ. He says that he is angry because God used him as a pawn and would not allow him into heaven, while Lucifer saw him as assisting God with His mighty plan and would not allow him in hell. Thus, he is cursed to roam the earth for eternity.

By the end of the movie, Judas asks for redemption and, ironically, is hung from a sign showing Christ hanging on the cross. The movie ends and allows the viewer to believe that his redemption was finally found and he was allowed to die. This movie was so popular that it continued with a second and third sequel.

Judas's story in pop culture is responsible for many of the beliefs that we have in vampire lore today. For example, vampires have repulsion to silver due to the fact that Judas sold his soul for thirty pieces of silver. They fear crucifixes, holy water, and other Christian symbols because they remind Judas of his betrayal of Christ.

And the most famous of the lore is that one can kill a vampire with a wooden stake made from the aspen tree. The aspen tree is known to be the tree that was used to make the cross that was used for crucifixion. But, many are not familiar with the fact that this is also the tree from which Judas attempted to hang himself, thus being the source of much pain in Christian lore.

All of these items have a central theme: Judas' repulsion of the symbols of his actions and his search for the answer of whether he acted of free will, of divine intervention, or of possession by Lucifer in regards to his role in the betrayal of Christ.

TNT's television series, *The Librarian,* completed the series with the movie *The Librarian: the Curse of the Judas Chalice.* In the series, the original vampire, Vlad the Impaler, is looking for the famed Judas chalice, which was used by Judas while consuming Jesus' "blood" at The Last Supper. The chalice was to heal the drinker and to grant power over all other vampires. Flynn Carson, the Librarian, goes through the movies spewing random information about vampires, their fear of crucifixes, holy water, etc. When he is engaged in the final battle with Vlad, he notices the aspen tree and realizes that his weapon is at his disposal. He explains the history of Judas' search for redemption as he kills Vlad and returns the chalice to the library.

Conclusion

The overall idea of the vampire is believed by many to be unchristian because it deals with demons and damnation. Van Helsing reiterates this belief in Dracula. He states that once a vampire bites and converts you, then you are the vampire and are one of the damned, no matter your circumstances. However, in the last decade, this view has changed drastically due to the huge presence of vampires in pop culture, represented in literature, movies, and role-playing games.

From the beginning of the search for empowerment with Lilith, to the search for acceptance with Cain, and the search for redemption with Judas, the use of the vampire in popular culture has allowed society to fulfill its need for religion. This lure of the vampire and the search of society for its specific need have brought about a strong connection that not only allows society to escape the mundane world around them, but to transcend to a level of the fulfillment of needs that each religious icon provides.

~~~VAMPIRES IN HISTORY~~~

Vlad Tepes! Elizabeth Bathory! Rod Ferrell! Each of these monsters has been labeled as a vampire in history. However, these monsters are not like the monsters on the pages of a book or scenes in a film, but instead are real life humans who have taken the form of a vampire in some role that they have played in their life.

Their gruesome acts have marked each a place in history as a vampiric monster- one who sucked the lives out of their victims either metaphorically or via blood drinking. But, no matter the outcome, their murdering sprees have forever named them as vampires in history.

~~Top 10 Vampire Killers in History~~

- Arnold Paole Meduegna –16th century – An Austrian legend about a Serbian man, Arnold, who came across a vampire one night and killed him. According to this legend, if you kill a vampire, then, when you die, you yourself became a vampire. Many years later, when the Serbian man died, he began roaming the village and killing people. The Austrian Army staked the corpse and he was never seen again.
- Countess Elizabeth Bathory –16th -17th century – The Hungarian cousin to Vlad Tepes made a murderous name for herself too. The countess was obsessed with her youthful looks, so much so that she killed thousands

- of girls to ensure that she could live eternally young and beautiful. It was said that one day she smacked one of her servants and blood ran upon her hand. As Elizabeth began to wipe it off, she found that it made her skin look younger. So, to keep her supply of beauty blood, she opened a finishing school for young peasant girls. But, when that supply ran out, she turned to the young aristocratic girls of the area. This was where she was caught. The peasant girls' families did not question them missing (many were hoping that they were married off to better families), but the aristocratic girls were missed. After a trial, she and her accomplices were found guilty. They were executed immediately, but because she was royalty, the countess was confined to her tower until her death, which was only four years later. Elizabeth has gained the title of the Blood or Vampire Queen because of her actions. Many of her people claim that this was just a story that was created to take the power and money from the young countess. Unfortunately, that cannot be proven.

- Gilles de Rais – 15th Century – Gilles was the war companion of Joan of Arc and was later charged as being one of the most prolific child serial killers in history. The victim count attributed to de Rais was just under 100 children. De Rais also dabbled in alchemy and magick. He was apprehended by the church with his "conspirators" and, after a "trial," was executed. He never confessed to the crime and, later, the Church was accused of charging him wrongly. After his death, the legend of his evil acts resulted in stories such as "Bluebeard."

- Manuela and Daniel Ruda – 1990-2000 – The European couple who killed friends to drink their blood. They met through an advertisement in a magazine that said, *"Black-haired vampire seeks princess of darkness who despises everything and everyone and has bidden farewell to life."* They chose one victim simply because he liked the Beatles and later claimed that Satan told them to do it. The police found body parts and blood lying outside their coffin in which they slept. They showed no remorse when they were arrested.

- Mercy Brown and the New England Vampire Craze – late 1700s to the 1800s – During the late 18th and early 19th centuries, there was a huge tuberculosis incident that occurred throughout New England. There were approximately twenty reports of family members who returned from the dead to drink the blood of and to kill other family members. The most famous was Mercy Brown who, according to court records, was exhumed for vampirism. The Brown family suffered from numerous losses like most families did during that time. The head of the Brown family, George, was compelled by the Town of Exeter to exhume the members of his family. When he unearthed his wife, son, and daughters, all but Mercy's body was decomposed. Her body was still full of blood and looked very much alive. She was blamed for the deaths of her family and the spread of vampirism. Her heart was removed and her body was burned. But, the true reason for her preservation was that Mercy had died later than those of her family and the cold winter weather affected the decomposition of her tissues to the point that she appeared untouched.

- Richard Chase – the Vampire of Sacramento – 1970s – Richard Chase's story was used to create the 1980s movie, *Unstoppable*. He started out killing animals and then progressed to killing humans. He had been witnessed by family members to be a danger to himself and animals, but was deemed "safe to society" on numerous occasions by experts. He was even institutionalized and was released to his parents as an adult. By the end of his reign, he was murdering and drinking the blood of his victims. One gruesome example was a pregnant woman whom he assaulted and mutilated, then cut out the baby, decapitated it, and drank its blood. He died Christmas, 1980.

• Rod Ferrell – 1996 – Rod Ferrell was a savage killer from Murray, Kentucky. He was great at manipulating his small group of outcast friends. He used the ruse of the White Wolf game, *Vampire Masquerade,* as a way of recruiting teens who wanted to live the vampire lifestyle. He told these other teens that his name was Vessago and that they were a part of his "Vampire Clan." They would experiment with drugs, drink, and, of course, complete blood exchange rituals. These teens left Kentucky to "rescue" Ferrell's girlfriend from her parents. He arrived in Florida and they brutally murdered the Wendorf family with a crowbar. There are many theories as to what exactly happened. During the trial, Scott Anderson, one of the young boys of the Vampire Clan, admitted to being with Ferrell when he killed the Wendorfs. The girls supposedly were not involved, but there is a question as to the guilt and involvement of the daughter, Heather. Some say that Heather asked Rod Ferrell to kill her parents, but during the trial, Ferrell said that the girls were not involved. The movie, *The Vampire Clan,* was based upon this incident. The two girls that came with Ferrell, Charity Keesee and Dana Cooper, were convicted of being accessories after the fact and each was sentenced to a ten-and-a-half-year prison sentence. Scott Anderson received life in prison without parole. Rod Ferrell was, at one time, the youngest person on death row at the age of 17, but in 1999, a Florida Appeals Court reduced his sentence to life without parole.

There is still a lot of speculation going around about what really may have happened and who really participated in what events. Because of the nature of this crime and the age of the participants, there may never be a clear cut sense of what happened on that evening.

- The Buckinghamshire Vampire – 12th Century – There was a vampire rumored to terrorize the Buckinghamshire area of England. He was one of the examples of a being who slept during the day and, at night, rose to terrorize his family, in this case specifically, his widow. The woman was so afraid that she asked to be kept awake and before long the whole town was scared to fall asleep. Finally, to end the spreading hysteria and the "terror" of the vampire, the townspeople disinterred him, placed a document upon his chest, and he never rose again.

- The Vampire of Berwick – 12th Century – William of Newburgh introduced this story of a vampire who terrorized the town of Berwick. The story tells of a man, held in high esteem in the town, who died. Upon his death, the villagers discovered that he was corrupt and evil, and decided not to allow him to be buried on consecrated ground. The next night, the villagers told stories of a man resembling him terrorizing the town and instances of the eating of the living. Supposedly, this townsman had dogs that followed him and barked as he did his untimely eating. Terrified, the town elders appointed ten men to raise the townsman's body from the ground, behead him, and burn the body. But, peace would not return to the town because after the Vampire of Berwick went through, a plague settled upon the city, killing most of its citizens.

- Vlad Tepes – 15th Century – Vlad Tepes, the Prince of Wallachia, became known as Vlad the Impaler. His full name was Vlad Dracul, meaning Vlad, Son of the Dragon. During his life, he defended his country against the Ottoman Turks. He used very sadistic and torturous methods such as "impaling" the bodies of his enemies around his castle as well as nailing their turbans to their heads. Even though his methods were horrific, his country believed him to be a savior of their freedom. He was credited with being the inspiration for Bram Stoker's *Dracula*. There are numerous documentaries about his life before he was prince, as well as after. Vlad is the historical vampire that everyone thinks of when they mention Dracula.

~~10 Historical Vampire Sites and Tours in Romania/Transylvania~~

- **Dracula Initiation Tours -**
  www.mysteriousjourneys.com
  They range from one day to several weeks. Prices vary
- **Dracula Sites in Transylvania via the Transylvanian Society of Dracula**
  http://www.ucs.mun.ca/~emiller/drac_romania.html
- **Dracula Tours -** www.dractours.com
  A week-long tour scheduled both during the summer and Halloween. These trips are limited to eighty people.
- **Go Romania Tours -** www.goromaniatours.com/ This is a mixture of the historical sites where Vlad lived and died as well as places referred to in Bram Stoker's book. For example, tourists can dine at the Golden Crown where Harker ate in the book. Price is based per person and is dependent upon hotel accommodations.
- **Romanian Tourism -** www.romaniatourism.com
  This is a list of places to visit compiled by the Romanian Tourism Department.
- **Tours of Romania -** http://www.romaniatours.us/
  There are guided tours as well as cultural retreats, home visits, and folklore performances. Prices vary.
- **Tours of Romania -** www.tours-of-romania.com
  They have a list of a three-day to eleven-day tour schedules.
- **Transylvania Live -** www.visit-transylvania.us
  These tours range from a few hours to a week with Vlad. They include Halloween parties, weekend excursions, historical excursions, and a visit to Vlad's supposed burial ground. Prices range from $200-$2000.

- **Transylvania Tours** - www.transylvania-tours.ro
  Day and week tours available at varying prices.
- **Transylvanian Castle** - www.transylvaniancastle.com
  Travel through the castles of Transylvania, including Vlad's castle. Tours include one day to two weeks and range in price up to around $1500 EU.

~~Vampire Monsters in Modern News~~

It appears that vampires are on the rise in the news, not as fictional characters, but as "monsters" in history. This year, there were many incidents that occurred that kept vampires in the news. These ranged from real life "vampire" graves being dug up, to actors being accused of being vampires, and the numerous incidents of vampire attacks throughout the country. Here are a few excerpts from my "Vampire Examiner" column.

Why the sudden unearthing of the vampire?

Over the past two and a half years, there have been several articles about the multiple "vampires" that have been dug up throughout the Bulgarian area. But, why now and why is it so important?

The most recent vampire skeleton was unearthed by Nikolay Ovcharov, an archaeologist in Bulgaria. This skeleton was tied down with four iron clamps.

Two bodies were found in an archaeological dig in Sozopol, according to history professor Bozhidar Dimitrov.

But, why is this so important? Why are they labeled as "vampires"? Many people have heard the story of Vlad the Impaler and his Wallachia home near Romania. They have heard of his very strong attacks against invaders into his country.

But, why are these vampires popping up and what happened in the Middle Ages in Eastern Europe? Simply, many people believed that when people died, that they might come back as vampires, especially if a cat jumped over the unburied body or they were not baptized.

Many would bury their dead upside down, on sacred ground, and stake them in the heart to attack them to the ground.

These bodies have been proven to be some of these people who were victims of this superstition. They were buried with stakes in their hearts or chained to their coffins.

Bulgaria's national history museum announced plans in 2012 of putting one of these bodies on display as a way of sharing the history of their country and their superstitions around vampires.

~ This is just one of hundreds of articles that have surfaced over the last five years. It is shocking to people only because the vampire is associated with this. These graves have been unearthed for years, but they have become more "vampire centered" since the vampire craze returned. ~

Man with vampire teeth attacks another homeless man

Well, we knew the narcissistic bloodsuckers couldn't stay out of the spotlight for too long and most vampires don't want to be outdone by zombies and their bath salt attacks, so we knew it was only a little while before vampires would be attacking homeless men too. And last year it happened, a homeless man with vampire teeth attacked another homeless man.

Early on a Wednesday morning, the San Diego Police Department received a phone call that an elderly transient gentleman was being bitten by another transient gentleman who had vampire teeth.

According to the U-T San Diego Newspaper, the fifty-five-year-old man said he was attacked in a shopping mall parking lot outside of CVS. He was wounded, but it was not life threatening.

They arrested the man with the vampire teeth, but no word yet as to his name or motive. The victim said he kicked the man several times because he was trying to kill him. The "vampire" man will be arrested for assault, but it may be upgraded to attempted murder, according to the SD police Captain, Brian Ahearn.

Well, if zombies weren't enough for you, now you got vampires roaming the street. Get your slaying kit now.

Vampire leads church blood drive and helps set church record on blood donations

In 2013, *The Telegraph*, Macon, Georgia's newspaper, reported that there was a vampire in their local church. George Ealer is called the local vampire at the Christ United Methodist Church, or so this is what the residents of a small town outside Macon, Georgia nicknamed him.

George moved from Pennsylvania to Georgia when he retired and moved to Warner Robins, Georgia to be closer to his son. While there, he started to look around for some things to volunteer for or to keep him busy. This is when he found that the blood drive coordinator had just quit and that his church was looking for a replacement.

He took the position as the blood donor coordinator and thought that it would be a very simple job, but the turnout was not so great. He then began to take matters into his own hands by thinking of how to creatively increase blood donations.

This creativity is what garnered him the name of the church vampire. One Sunday, before the church's blood drive, Ealer came dressed as a vampire. He had the full cape and all and sat down in the front pew at church. He then gave a great invitation to the church members to the upcoming church blood drive.

Their first blood drive, when Ealey took over, only brought in 133 units of blood. Since then, Ealey and his creativity has more than tripled the blood donations at the church's blood drive.

This last year, it was 586 units and the blood drive is currently going on this week. They are hoping to break their record and to continue to help with those that are in need of blood.

So, what do you think about this creative way of getting people to donate blood?

Kuddos to him and his creativity and to the church for being so open to this fun way of promoting this event.

~Did You Know?~

- More couples who have been labeled as vampire killers have met over the Internet by being honest about what they are looking for – someone to help them kill and drink someone else's blood.

- Fritz Haarmann, known the Vampire of Hanover, is labeled a serial killer for his twenty-seven murders. His brain is now preserved in a jar in the Gottingen Medical School so that it can be studied.

- Throughout history, many females have been blamed for being vampires just like they have been labeled as witches. It was not uncommon throughout history to find women buried with rocks and stones lodged in their mouths because the townspeople thought that this would keep the "vampire" from eating the plague victims or attacking the living.

- Just like in mythology, there is a vampire serial killer in most of the major cultures of the world. Makes you wonder, doesn't it, just how much influence the vampire really has in this world.

~~~VAMPIRES IN LITERATURE~~~

Vampires entered the literary world in the 1800s. They began as monsters that struck fear into the hearts of the reader. Varney and Lord Ruthven were the first to introduce what many call the "traditional" vampire, the monster who was so tormented and embraced the idea that he was a vampire. He knew who he was and accepted it.

Bram Stoker was the first to introduce vampires as scary but sexually appealing. Dracula brought sex to the Victorian world, which was very shocking for that time. The exchange of blood and Mina nursing from his chest were very erotic scenes.

The second book was *Carmilla* and the introduction of female love and attraction. LeFanu painted a very erotic picture, using the power of words to conjure vivid images in our mind. The early vampire literature was full of passion, forbidden love, and social commentary that allowed the vampire to enter the home of readers and to create fans that would last centuries.

Authors like Anne Rice and Charlaine Harris are now introducing new generations to vampires. Their vampires are romantic, aristocratic, but very much still the vampire that was created in the 19th century. But, they are still monsters who accept their undead lives as vampires and lure us into the books just as Stoker, LeFanu, Prest, Polidori, and Byron did so many years ago and still do today.

~~The Beginning of Vampires in Print~~

Most are in public domain and available here-
www.gutenberg.org

First poems or short stories

- "The Vampire" by Heinrich August Ossenfelder 1748
- "Lenore" by Gottfried August Bürger 1773
- "Die Braut von Corinth The Bride of Corinth" by Johann Wolfgang von Goethe 1797
- "Thalaba the Destroyer" by Robert Southey1801
- "The Vampyre" by John Staggs 1810
- "The Spectral Horseman" by Percy Bysshe Shelley 1810
- "Ballad in St. Irvyne" by Percy Bysshe Shelley 1811
- Samuel Taylor Coleridge's unfinished "Christabel" 1813
- "The Giaour" by Lord Byron 1813
- *Vampyre* by John Polidori 1819 novella

Literary Books
- *La Morte Amoureuse* by Théophile Gautier 1836
- *The Family of the Vourdalak* by Count Alexis Tolstoy 1843
- *Varney the Vampire or The Feast of Blood* by James Malcolm Rymer or Thomas Peckett Prest 1847
- *Le Chevalier Ténèbre (Knightshade)* by Paul Féval 1860
- *La Vampire (The Vampire Countess)* by Paul Féval 1865

- *Carmilla* by Sheridan le Fanu 1872
- *La Ville Vampire (Vampire City)* by Paul Féval 1874
- *After Ninety Years* by Milovan Glišić 1880
- *The Fate of Madame Cabanel* by Eliza Lynn Linton 1880
- *Manor* by Karl Heinrich Ulrichs 1884
- *The True Story of the Vampire* by Count Stanislaus Eric Stenbock 1894
- *Lilith* by George MacDonald 1895
- *Dracula* by Bram Stoker 1897

~~10 Vampiric Characteristics of Bram Stoker's *Dracula*~~

- Can crawl down walls and shape shift into animals.
- Can control humans, animals, and weather and can turn into vapor, fog, bats, and wolves.
- Cannot cross water at low and high tide or enter someone's home without permission.
- Is repelled by garlic crucifixes and Eucharist bread and to be staked is the ultimate way to death.
- Has no pulse/heartbeat and is cold to the touch. Has very bad breath and long fingernails.
- Has no shadow or reflection.
- Must sleep in his native soil.
- Has night vision.
- Can walk in the sun. It only weakens him. He can only transform at dawn, noon, and dusk.
- Can change humans to vampires and lives as a loner with mates, but not other vampires or in covens.

∼∼10 Vampire Characteristic Firsts in Literature∼∼

- Vampire to die in the sun – Count Orlock – *Nosferatu* – 1922
- Vampire that had protruding fangs – Varney – *Varney the Vampire* –1845-1847
- Vampire that had mesmerizing eyes – Varney – *Varney the Vampire* –1845- 1847
- Vampire to be healed in the moonlight – Lord Ruthen – *The Vampyre* – 1819
- Vampire described as having mesmerizing beauty Carmilla – *Carmilla* – 1871
- Vampire book that introduced the idea of no reflection or no shadow, shape shifting and flying Dracula – *Dracula* – 1897
- Vampire to wear a cloak – Dracula – Stage productions of *Dracula* – 1920s
- Children's vampire – Bunnicula – *Bunnicula* –1971
- Vampire Muppet – Count von Count – *Sesame Street* – 1972
- Sparkly vampire – *Twilight* by Stephenie Meyer – 2005

∼∼Did You Know? ∼∼

- Did you know that the reason for the vampire cape came about in the theater adaptations of *Dracula* to help Bela Lugosi "disappear"?

- Did you know that the literary characters Lord Ruthven and Varney could be healed in the moonlight?

- Did you know that *Varney the Vampire* was a penny dreadful which meant that the cost for the continuing weekly story was just a penny? The stories were focused on the working class patrons and many times were terribly written.

- Did you know that there are multiple interpretations of Bram Stoker's *Dracula,* which include it being a Christian metaphor, a social political piece on sex, and about xenophobia, feminism, and disease? Even today, scholars are still studying *Dracula* to find additional meanings for the Victorian novel.

- Did you know that Bram Stoker was the assistant to Henry Irving, the owner of the Lyceum Theater?

- Did you know that the vampire has evolved over the last few decades to include not only the monsters that survive on blood, but those that are like aliens and feed off the energy of their hosts?

- Many people want to blame modern literature for the romanticizing of the vampire, but in truth, vampires were erotic and sexual beings even in the literature of the 1800s.

- Did you know that Elizabeth Caroline Grey was the first woman to have her vampire story published? It was in 1828 and was called *The Skeleton Count* or *The Vampire Mistress.*

~~Young Adult Vampire Books~~

- A Furry Fable Series by Veronica Blade
- Angel Creek Series by Ada Adams
- *A Shade of Vampire* by Bella Forrest
- Batman: Vampire Series by Doug Moench
- *Bite Me!* by Melissa Francis
- *Blood Moon* by Robin P. Waldrop
- *Blood of Eden* by Julie Kagawa
- Blood of Darkness Series by Richard S. Hartmetz
- Bloodline Series by Kare Cary
- *Bloodlines* by Lindsay Anne Kendal
- *Bloodstained Oz* by Christopher Golden and James Moore
- Blue Bloods Series by Melissa de la Cruz
- Brookehaven Vampires Series by Joann Martin Sowles
- *Cirque Du Freak: The Vampire's Assistant* by Daren Shan
- *Cody Blanchard Series by Serena Robar*
- *Companions of the Night* by Vivian Vande Velde
- *Dangerous Girls* by R.L. Stine
- *Darke Academy* by Gabriella Poole
- *Evernight* by Claudia Gray
- Fallen Series by Lauren Kate
- Good Ghouls Series by Julie Kenner
- *High School Bites* by Liza Conrad
- *iDrakula* by Bekka Black
- *Infinite Days* by Rebecca Maizel
- *Insatiable* by Meg Cabot
- *Isaac* by P.H. Dillard
- *Josie Griffin Is Not a Vampire* by Heather Swain
- *Kiss of Death* by Jayme and Judy Morse

- *Modern Marvels – Viktoriana* by Wayne Reinagel
- Moogie Chronicles by Morgan Routh
- Moth Series by Karen Mahoney
- Multiple Vampire Series by Katie Maxwell
- Multiple Vampire Titles by Amelia Atwater Rhoads
- *My Blood Approves* by Amanda Hocking
- *Night Huntress* by Jeaniene Frost
- *Nightworld* by L. J. Smith
- *Peeps* by Scott Westerfeld
- School for Vampires series by Jackie Niebisch
- *Still Sucks to Be Me: The All-True Confessions of Mina Smith, Teen Vampire* by Kimberly Paule
- *Strange Angels* by Lili St. Crow, Lilith Saintcrow
- *Suck it Up* by Brian Meehl
- *Sucks to be Me* by Kimberly Pauley
- *Sweet Blood* by Pete Hautman
- Talisman Series by Brenda Pandos
- *Tantalize* by Cynthia Leitich Smith
- The Alexa Montgomery Saga by H.D. Gordon
- *The Blood Coven* by Mari Mancusi
- *The Captive* by Erica Stevens
- *The Cheerleader* by Caroline B. Cooney
- The Darkangel series by Meredith Ann Pierce
- *The Dark Heroine* by Abigail Gibbs
- The Den of Shadows Quartet Series by Amelia Atwater-Rhodes
- The Hollows Series by Kim Harrison
- The House of Night Series by P. C. Cast & Kristin Cast
- The Hunt Series by Andrew Fukuda
- *The Last Days* by Scott Westerfeld
- The Last Vampire Series by Christopher Pike
- *The Last Vampire* by Willis Hall
- *The Many Faces of Van Helsing* by Jeanne Cavelos

- *The Morganville Vampires* by Rachel Caine
- *The Reformed Vampire Support Group* by Catherine Jinks
- The Royal Blood Chronicles by Elizabeth Loraine
- *The Silver Kiss* by Annette Curtis Klause
- *The Sorcery Code by Dima Zales*
- The Twilight Series by Stephenie Meyer
- *The Vampire Academy* by Richelle Mead
- *The Vampire Diaries* by L. J. Smith
- *The Vampire Princess* by Tate Halloway
- The Vampires of Manhattan: The New Blue Bloods Coven by Melissa de la Cruz
- *Therian* by Leandi Cameron
- *Thicker than Water* by Carla Jablonski
- *Thirst* by Christopher Pike
- *Thirsty* by M.T. Anderson
- *Uninvited* by Amanda Marrone
- *Vampirates* by Justin Somper
- Vampire Beach Series by Alex Duval
- Vampire Empire Series by Stella Purple
- *Vampire Formula* by Paul Andrew Ross
- *Vampire High* by Douglass Rees
- *Vampire Haiku* by Ryan Mecum
- Vampire Kisses Series by Ellen Schreiber
- *Vampire Manifest* by Rashasad Bell
- Vampires of Manhattan by Melissa dela Cruz
- *Vampires Rule* by K. C. Blake
- Vladimir Todd Series by Heather Brewer
- What You See is What You Get Series by Nicole Zoltack

~~Adult Vampire Books~~

- *A Vampire's Vedas* by Antoinette Medina
- *Abraham Lincoln Vampire Hunter* by Seth Grahame-Smith
- *Alraune* by Hans Heinz Ewers
- *Amaranthine Series* by Joleene Naylor
- *And Dark My Desire and And Darker My Wrath* by John Schreiber
- Anita Blake: Vampire Hunter Series by Laurell K. Hamilton
- Anna Strong Series by Jeanne C. Stein
- Anno Dracula Series by Kim Newman
- Barnabas Collins Series by Marilyn Ross
- *Between Shadows* by Joanne Duran
- *Bewitched by Edith Wharton*
- Bite Me! A Love Story Series by Christopher Moore
- *Blood and Whiskey* by Clark Hays and Kathlene McFall
- Blood Books Series by Tanya Huff
- *Blood Circle* by P.N. Elrod
- *Blood Junky* by Stavros
- *Blood Oath* by Christopher Farnsworth
- *Blood Prophecy: The Fated Three* by T.L. Spencer
- Bloodwine Series by Freda Warrington
- *Breathless* by Scott Prussing
- Brytewood Series by Rosemary Laurey writing as Georgia Evans
- *Carpe Jugulum* by Terry Pratchett
- *Children of the Night* by Dan Simmons
- *Crimson Shadow* by Nathan Squiers
- *Danilov Quintet* by Jasper Kent
- Dark Kiss Trilogy by Liz Strange

- Dark Series by Christine Feehan
- Dark-Hunter Series by Sherrilyn Kenyon
- *Dead and Loving It* by Mary Janice Davidson
- Dead Walker Series by Angelique Armae
- Dearg-Sidhe Series by S.P. Hendrick
- *Deeply Rooted* by C.C. Rogers and A.L. Moffitt
- *Dhamphir* by Scott Baker
- *Dracula in Love* by Karen Essex
- *Dracula the Un-Dead* by Dacre Stoker
- *Dracula the Undead* by Freda Warrington
- *Dracula's Guest* by Bram Stoker
- *Dracula's Guest* by Michael Sims
- *Eighteen Everlasting* by Tracey Stoltman
- *Empire V* by Victor Pelevin
- *Eternal Desire* and other vampire titles by Roxanne Rhoads
- *Fangland* by John Marks
- *Fangs Rule* by Amy Mah
- *Fat Vampire:* A Never Coming of Age Story by Adam Rex
- *Fevre Dream* by George R. R. Martin
- *Fledgling* by Octavia Butler
- *For the Blood is the Life* by F. Marion Crawford
- *Forever Vampires* by Rosemary Laurey
- *I Am Legend* by Richard Matheson
- Immortyl Revolution Series by Denise Verrico
- Immortyl Series by Paul Lewis
- Imprinted Souls Series by Daniele Lanzarotta
- *In the Diaries of the Family Dracul* by Jeanne Kalogridis
- *Insatiable* by Meg Cabot
- Jane Jameson Series by Molly Harper
- *Judgement of Souls* by Margarita Felices

- *Killer Kisses* by Chastity Bush
- *Knight of the Black Rose* by James Lowder
- *Lady Christina* by Mircea Eliade
- *Let the Right One In* by John Ajvide Lindqvist
- *Lillian* by Elizabeth Loraine
- *Lost Souls* by Poppy Z. Brite
- Love at Stake Series by Kerrilyn Sparks
- Macedo Ink Series-by BittenTwice
- *Magnetic* by Marja Healy
- Midnight Breed Series by Lara Adrian
- *Mina: the Stoker Story Continues* by Marie Kiraly
- *Modern Marvels - Viktoriana* by Wayne Reinagel
- Multiple Vampire Books by Kate Hill
- Multiple Vampire Books by Michele Hauf
- My Sister the Vampire Series by Sienna Mercer
- Night Huntress Series by Jeaniene Frost
- *Pages from a Young Girl's Journal* by Robert Aickman
- *Pandora* by Anne Rice
- *Past Due* by C.S. Winchester
- *Peeps* by Scott Westerfield
- Prince Eternal Series by Monique Marie
- *Ravenna and the Resurrected* by Tami Jackson
- Real Vampires Series by Gerry Bartlett
- *Relations that Suck* by Marilyn Yu
- *Release* by Nicole Hadaway
- *Renfield: Slave of Dracula* by Barbara Hambly
- *Revelations in Black* by Carl Jacobi
- Saint-Germain Series by Chelsea Quinn Yarbro
- Saints and Shadows Saga by Christopher Golden
- *Salem's Lot* by Stephen King
- *Shadow Dwellers* by J. C. Wilder
- *Shattered Glass* by Elaine Bergstroms
- *Some of Your Blood* by Theodore Sturgeon

- *Son of Air and Darkness Series* by S.P. Hendrick
- *Sunglasses of the Dark* by Nancy Collins
- *Sunshine* by Robin McKinley
- Texas Vampire Series by Diane Whiteside
- *The Adventure of the Sussex Vampire* by Sir Arthur Conan Doyle
- The Black Castle Series by Les Daniels
- The Black Dagger Brotherhood Series by JR Ward
- The Calling Series by Caridad Piñeiro
- The Carpathian Series by Christine Feehan
- *The Case of the Sanginarian Count* by Loren D. Estlemans
- The Circle Trilogy by Nora Roberts
- *The Cowboy and The Vampire* by Clark Hays and Kathlene McFall
- *The Dark Castle* by Marion Brandon
- The Dead Series by Tate Hallaway
- *The Dracula Poems* by Robin Sprigg
- *The Dracula Tapes* by Fred Saberhagan
- *The Dragon Waiting* by John M. Ford
- *The Dresden Files* by Jim Butcher
- *The Flowering of the Strange Orchid* by H. G. Wells. 1894
- *The Girl with the Hungry Eyes* by Fritz Leiber
- *The Historian* by Elizabeth Kostova
- *The Holmes Dracula Files* by Haber Saberhagan
- *The House of the Vampire* by George Sylvester Viereck
- *The Hunger* by Whitley Strieber
- *The Informers* by Brett Easton Ellis
- *The Keep* by F. Paul Wilson
- *The Lair of the White Worm* by Bram Stoker
- *The Last Vampire* by Christopher Pike
- *The Light at the End* by John Skipp and Craig Spector

- *The Longest Night* by Ray Russell
- *The Necroscope Saga* by Brian Lumley
- *The Night Flyer* by Stephen King
- *The Night Outside* by Ardeth Alexander
- *The Primes Universe* by Susan Sizemore
- *The Renquist Quartet* by Mick Farren
- *The Room in the Tower* by E.F. Benson
- *The Silver Kiss* by Annette Curtis Klause
- *The Sin Eater's Prince* by Keta Diablo
- The Sookie Stackhouse Series by Charlaine Harris
- The Stoker Sisters Series by Kailin Gow
- *The Stress of Her Regard* by Tim Powers
- The Templar Vampire Series by Rene Lyons
- *The Tomb of Sarah* by F. G. Loring
- The Undead and Unwed Series by Mary Janice Davidson
- The Vampire Huntress Series by L. A. Banks
- The Vampire Shrink Series by Lynda Hilburn
- *The Vampire Sonnets* by David Bradsher
- *They Thirst* by Robert McCammon
- *Thicker than Water* by Greg Sicso
- *Those Who Hunt the Night (UK title: Immortal Blood)* by Barbara Hambly
- *Travelling with the Dead* by Barbara Hambly
- *Under the Moon* by Kristie O' Toole
- Vampire Chronicles Series by Anne Rice
- Vampire Earth Series by E.E.Knight
- Vampire Files Series by P.N. Elrod
- Vampire Inn Series by C.J. Ellisson
- *Vampire of the Mists* by Christie Golden
- Vampire Queen Series by Joey W Hill
- Vampire Series by Angela Knight
- *Vampire$* by John Steakley

- *Vampire's Most Wanted* by Laura Enright
- *Vampires Romance to Rippers: An Anthology of Tasty Stories* by Scarlette D' Noir et al
- *Vampires Romance to Rippers: An Anthology of Risque Stories* by Scarlette D' Noir etal
- *Wampir (The Vampire)* by Władysław Reymont
- Wings in the Night Series by Maggie Shayne

~~Short Stories~~

- "A Princess of Darkness" by Frederick Cowles
- "Descent into Egypt" by Algernon Blackwood
- "John Barrington Cowles" by Sir Arthur Conan Doyle
- "Terror of the Twins" by Algernon Blackwood
- "The Dracula Book of Great Vampire Stories" by Leslie Shepard
- "The Last Lords of Gardonae" by William Gilbert
- "The Paleface Lady" by Alexandre Dumas
- "The Parasite" by Sir Arthur Conan Doyle
- "The Transfer" by Algernon Blackwood
- "Weird War Tales" by Arnold Drake and Tony de Zuniga
- "With Intent to Steal" by Algernon Blackwood

~~Manga and Anime~~

- *A Dark Rabbit Has Seven Lives*
- *A House in Venice*
- *Black Blood Brothers*
- *Blade*
- *Blood Alone*

- *Blood Hound*
- *Blood Lad*
- *Blood Soul*
- *Blood Sucker: Legend of Zipangu*
- *Blood: The Last Vampire*
- *Blood+*
- *Blood-C*
- *Blood Sucker*
- *Bloody Kiss*
- *Canon*
- *Chibi Vampire*
- *China Blue Jasmine*
- *Chu Chu Chu*
- *Cirque de Freak*
- *Crepiscule*
- *Crescent Moon*
- *Crimson Cross*
- *Dance in the Vampire Bund*
- *Dark Edge*
- *Dark Hunters*
- *Darren Shan*
- *Descendants of Darkness*
- *Devil May Cry*
- *D-Gray-Man*
- *Diabolik Lovers*
- *Digimon*
- *Digimon Adventures 1 and 2*
- *Digimon Data Squad*
- *Don Dracula*
- *Dracu-Riot!*
- *Dracula: Sovereign of the Dammed*
- *Endo Beast*
- *Fortune Arterial*

- *Gesshoku no Cavalier*
- *Gregory's Horror Show*
- *Hellsing*
- *Hellsing Ultimate*
- *Hellsing: New Dawn*
- *Higanjima*
- *Hipira: The Little Vampire*
- *Hitsuji no Uta*
- *Holy Knight*
- *Interview with the Vampire*
- *Itsuka Tenma no Kuro Usagi*
- *Jack Frost*
- *JoJo's Bizarre Adventure*
- *Junketsut Karesh*
- *Kanpail*
- *Karin*
- *Kesshoku no Shugosha*
- *Kigeki*
- *Kimera*
- *Kuro Bara Alice*
- *Kurozuka*
- *Kyuuketsuhime Miyu*
- *Kyuuketsuhim Yui: Kanoshou*
- *Kyuuketsuki to Boku*
- *Kyuuketsu Yuugi*
- *Lament of the Lamb*
- *Legend of Duo*
- *Long Along Alonging*
- *Love Monster*
- *Lunar Legend Tsukihime*
- *Magical Pokan*
- *Master Mosquiton*
- *Midnight Hunters*

- *Midnight Secretary*
- *Millennium Snow*
- *MitsuAji Blood*
- *Mitsukazu Mihara: Beautiful People*
- *Model*
- *Moon Phase*
- *My Boyfriend is A Vampire*
- *Nanchatte Vampiyan*
- *Nekrateholic*
- *Negima!*
- *New Vampire Miyu*
- *Night Exile*
- *Nightmare Syndrome*
- *Night Warriors: Darkstalkers' Revenge*
- *Nightwalker: The Midnight Detective*
- *Noblesse*
- *Nyanpire The Animation*
- *Omae ga Sekai wo Kowashitai nara*
- *Orange Marmalade*
- *OVA*
- *Princess Resurrection*
- *Rebirth*
- *Record of a Fallen Vampire*
- *Renkin Sankyu Magical? Pokan*
- *Rosario+ Vampires*
- *Sequences*
- *Sfumare*
- *Shaman King*
- *Sheep's Song*
- *Shiki*
- *Shingetsutan Tsukihime*
- *Strike The Blood*
- *Sword of the Dark Ones*

- *The Record of a Fallen Vampires*
- *The Vampire Dahlia*
- *The Wandered*
- *Tokimeki Tonight*
- *Trinity Blood*
- *Tsukihime*
- *Tsukuyomi: Moon Phase*
- *Ultraviolet: Code 044*
- *Until the Full Moon*
- *UQ Holder!*
- *Valvave the Liberator*
- *Vampi*
- *Vampire Academy*
- *Vampire Crisis*
- *Vampire Doll Guilt na Zan*
- *Vampire Game*
- *Vampire Girl*
- *Vampire Host*
- *Vampire Hunter D*
- *Vampire Hunter D: Bloodlust*
- *Vampire Juuikai*
- *Vampire Kisses*
- *Vampire Knight*
- *Vampire Princess Miyu*
- *Vampire Savior*
- *Vampire Vampire!*
- *Vampire Yui*
- *Vampire Wars*
- *Vampiyan Kids*
- *Vassalord*
- *Wallachia*
- *Yami no Teio: Kyuuketsuki Dracula*
- *Yato no Kamitsukai*

- *Yoake no Vampire*
- *Yui Komon*

~~Comics and Graphic Novels~~

- *30 Days of Night* – IDW
- *American Gothic*
- *American Vampire* – DC
- *Angel* – Dark Horse
- *Anita Blake: Vampire Hunter* – Dark Horse
- *Astro City* – Vertigo
- *Baltimore* – Dark Horse
- *Batman: Bloodstorm* – DC
- *Batman: Crimson Mist* – DC
- *Batman and Dracula Red Rain* – DC
- *Bethany Vampfire* – Brainstorm Comics
- *Bite Club* – Vertigo
- *Black Kiss* – Vorrtex
- *Blade* – Marvel
- *Bloody Mary* – DC
- *Bloodstrom* – Marvel
- *Buffy the Vampire Slayer* – Dark Horse
- *Crimson – Images and* DC
- *Dark Shadows* – Dynamite Entertainment
- *Dark Shadows* – Gold Key Comics
- *Death of Dracula* Marvel
- *Death Ship* – IDW
- *Dracula* – Marvel
- *Dracula vs. King Arthur*
- *Dracula* – Dell Comics
- *Dracula's Guest* – Dynamite Entertainment
- *Exodus* – Marvel

- *Giant Size Dracula –* Marvel
- *Guilty Pleasures –* Marvel
- *Hellsing* – Dark Horse
- *I am Legion* – DC
- *I, Vampire –* DC
- *Kristina Queen of the Vampires* by Frans Mensink
- *Legion of Monsters –* Marvel
- *Le Morte' Sisters*
- *Life Sucks by Jessica Abel –* First Second Comics
- *Lilith, Daughter of Dracula –* Marvel
- *Looker –* DC
- *Monk: Batman –* DC
- *Morbius, the Living Vampire –* Marvel
- *Nancy Drew Vampire Slayer –* Papercutz
- *Pinocchio the Vampire Slayer Series –* SLG Publishing
- *Preacher –* DC
- *Stoker's Dracula –* Marvel
- *Sword of Dracula –* Image Comics
- *The Lost Boys: Reign of Frogs –* Wildstorm
- *The New Deadwardians –* Vertigo
- *The Vampire Huntress –* Marvel
- *Tomb of Dracula –* Marvel
- *True Blood –* HBO
- *Twilight: The Graphic Novel –* Little Brown
- *Vampire Academy by Richelle Mead –* Penguin Books
- *Vampire Kisses*
- *Vampirella –* Dynamite Entertainment
- *Vampire Rock*
- *Varnae –* Marvel
- *X – Men Apocalypse versus Dracula –* Marvel

Bertena Varney, M.A., M.Ed.

~~Magazines~~

- *Bite Me - bitememagazine.com*
- *Gothic Beauty - gothicbeauty.com*
- *Carpe Nocturne Magazine - carpenocturne.net*
- *Cult Vampire Magazine - bbc.co.uk/cult/vampires/*
- *Dark Discoveries - darkdiscoveries.com*
- *Horror Hound – horrorhound.com*
- *Vampiria Magazine - castleofvampiria.com/*
- *Hungur Magazine - sdpbookstore.com/hungur.htm*
- *IndieJudge Magazine - indiejudge.com*

~~ Did You Know?~~

- James Marsters, who played the hot vampire Spike on both the Buffy the Vampire Slayer series and its spin-off, *Angel* does the voices for the audio books for The Dresden Files and The Greyfriar Series. The Greyfriar Series is a new steampunk vampire trilogy that was written by Clay and Susan Smith. The first book is titled *Vampire Empire,* the second is *The Rift Walker,* and the third is *The Kingmakers.*

He also voices Melissa Marr's new Carnival of Souls series. Look for James's voice on more upcoming books and movies too. If you would like to contact him, he can be found at www.jamesmarsterslive.com or on twitter @jm¬_live.

~The Vampire's Influence on Teenage Self Identification~

As children grow into teenagers, they begin a search for self-identity. They look to others for acceptance and guidelines, but also want to be independent from their family and friends. For many teenagers, this means learning lessons the same way that they have since birth, through pop culture and the media.

Teens suffer from unwilling physical changes, new desires that they do not understand, and problems they have never faced, and they face all of this with a sense of immortality. They are filled with confusion, ambiguity, and fear of the future. According to James DeMarco's article "Vampire Literature: Something Young Adults Can Really Sink Their Teeth Into," literature remains a source of example and comfort to teens.

Teens can use the characters in books to try on different personas and even live out social taboos through fantasy. They can then begin to develop a sense of identity and even resolve everyday problems of acceptance, abuse, purpose in life, need for stability, and peer pressure. De Marco states that the perfect genre of literature that gratifies and indulges the teen's narcissistic needs is vampire literature.

For his article, he interviewed Dr. James Twitchell, a noted literary scholar, about the idea of the popularity of the vampire among teenagers. Dr. Twitchell states that vampires do not have identity crises or suffer from them too long; they know who and what they are and, many times, they are trying to work this out in the story. However, in the end, they are still confident, immortal, strong, and intelligent. Teens know that every goal the vampire desires can be reached, unlike their own frightful futures.

Christine Meloni, author of the article, "The Rise of Vampire Literature," believes that young adult vampire literature is very thought-provoking and character driven. According to Meloni, many people feel as if the genre is too gothic and dark, but Meloni argues that it is a mixture of romance, mystery, and humor. She describes many of her readers as "castaway students," meaning that if a book doesn't grab their attention and they cannot relate to it within the first few pages, then they will cast the book away.

With the recent popularity of movies such as the *Twilight Saga* and television shows such as *The Vampire Diaries,* many question if teens are not only using the plot to work out their social issues, but are instead losing their identities.

Today, sales in literature and the relationship that the vampire gives to the teenage reader are still on the rise. A few of the top book series of this genre are: Vampire Kisses by Ellen Schreiber, Blue Bloods by Melissa de La Cruz, and Twilight by Stephenie Meyer.

Each, in its unique way, relates to a different type of teenager. Vampire Kisses is written more for the outsider that is still insecure in who she is. Blue Bloods *is* written for the teen that loves fashion, modeling, and shopping while trying to decide who they can trust. And finally, Twilight, relates to not only the girl next door or the awkward teenage girl, but also to their mothers who are many times readers of vampire romance and want to share this newfound interest with their daughters.

The first series, Vampire Kisses, relates more to its gothic readers. The main character is sixteen-year-old Raven, a non-conformist who is attracted to a boy at school who turns out to be a vampire. She is a younger character who still relies upon her family and friends for her boundaries and identity. She searches for acceptance while fighting the bad vampires who want to harm her family and friends.

The story is fun and adventurous. It is a mixture of a teen's learning to trust others while finding someone who accepts you for you. Vampire Kisses is a simple read that can be used as an introduction to the vampire genre as well as an introduction to young adult literature.

The second series is Blue Bloods. These stories are written for the teen reader who enjoys shopping and the country club scene. The vampires in this book are the world's wealthy and beautiful teenagers in their private New York school.

Schuyler Van Allen is the newest student to this elite group. But all is not perfect in their world. Once they reach a certain age, they are transformed into vampires with fashion and attitude.

The author, Melissa de La Cruz, created them as once fallen angels who are now vampires on this earth. They must continue to reincarnate into a human body until each has been redeemed or lives out their life cycle.

The story tells of each character's search for who they were in their past life as well as whom they are to become in this life. The readers identify with her struggle to fit in, the acceptance and rejection by the peers, as well as the mystery and adventure of who the silver bloods are that are killing these new vampires. The Blue Bloods Series introduces the mystery and self-exploration that is true to this new genre.

The final series to be discussed is the most famous of the three: Twilight. The story is told as first-person narrative through the main character, Bella Swan.

Bella is a plain girl-next-door who meets and falls in love with the most beautiful vampire in the world, or in their world, Edward Cullen. Teen girls identify with Bella's average life. It is a Romeo and Juliet story where the two are drawn together by fate while trying to manage their relationship as human and vampire.

Twilight is a different vampire story than those in the past. The author, Stephenie Meyer, is a devout Mormon. Her religious views can be seen in the fact that Meyer's vampires don't show fangs and are self-proclaimed vegetarians (they live off the blood of animals, not humans).

But the biggest difference in this story is that the vampires hide from the sunlight not because they will turn to dust, but because they will sparkle like diamonds. They are perfect creatures.

However, the story is not a simple happy one. It is wrought with Edward's desire to kill Bella the first time they meet and Bella's struggle between her love for Edward and her friendship with Jacob, a werewolf and a member of the enemy clan of the Cullen family. There is discussion by readers about Edward's activity being a stalking of Bella, Bella's loss of identity when she is with Edward, the characters' discussion of abortion and, of course, the controversial underlying abstinence lesson that results in a heavy sex scene in the last book, only after they are married. These are all topics that are prevalent in the world of teenagers today.

Many of the *Twilight* fans are as young as nine, and this is their first introduction to being a teenager and how teenagers deal with relationships. They have had fairytales read to them as a child and these young adult books are a means to live out their teen fantasies, their new image of the perfect "bad boy" or the perfect "Prince Charming." The books become these children's guidebook, whether they are aware of it or not.

Today, vampires in young adult literature are fixtures in youth's lives. Teens spend more of their time either watching television or reading than two generations earlier. Many are home alone due to working parents and have entertained themselves with these two examples of pop culture. A popular sociological theory, structural functionalism, states that people learn through social institutions such as family and culture and, when one is absent, the other steps in to fill the void. As a result, literature of popular culture becomes the teacher of today's youth. The vampire was introduced to these youth at an early age and has maintained strong staying power. It is only natural that it may become the role model for teen's socialization whether it is learning to make friends, find acceptance, or make life choices.

~The Lure of the Dead Boyfriend~

In the beginning, there was a bald monster with a long face, pointed ears and chin, elongated fingers, and sharp talon claws, which lost its humanity and control over its monstrous side. It was lured to a young maiden's window. All of a sudden, with a sudden rush that could not be foreseen and with a strange howling cry that was enough to awaken the terror in any beast, the figure seized the long tresses of hair. He held her to the bed…she screamed…shrieked…and he seized her neck in his fang-like teeth... a gush of blood and a hideous sucking noise followed.

This picture of rape and torture is the bedroom scene of the 1847 penny dreadful, *Varney the Vampire: Feast of Blood.* The author, Thomas Prest, painted pictures of the vampire being a sexual monster who wanted to devour women – women who were portrayed as being very passive and weak. In these stories, the vampire bite was a metaphor for rape and the monster wanted his victim aware of every agonizing violation. This was the vampire that was created when men ruled the horror world: a creature cursed to walk the earth for eternity searching not for love, but for food.

Now, today, the story reads more like this: *"He met my eyes with his penetrating gaze. Suddenly, it was hard to breathe. My heart pounded in my chest... my knees threatened to buckle. I had never seen such a gorgeous man...something about him felt dark and dangerous and desirable. I lifted my chin to give him better access to my neck. He smiled, showing a hint of fangs."* This excerpt is from Lynda Hilburn's *The Vampire Shrink.* Lynda discussed on her blog that since women have taken over the horror genre, the vampire has evolved into a gorgeous, sensuous, sexual, romantic, bad boy of the night.

Even though vampire literature is usually snubbed by many writers and readers of the horror genre, over the last ten years, the rise in vampire literature has increased exponentially. Many book reviewers claim that vampire literature displays women as slutty and submissive. This may be true in some series, but overall, this trend has changed quickly. Many writers, such as C.J. Ellisson, author of The Vampire Vacation Series, have developed a strong, empowered female character that is a monogamous vampire who loves her human husband. The scenes are hot, but very respectful to women and actually show how they may embrace their sexual side without embarrassment.

Many more vampire authors have their female character as empowering and strong. They walk alongside the vampire in their journey rather than being the damsel in distress or the hapless victim of his sexual prowess. The current trend for this new genre of vampire romance literature is one that offers the readers an escape from the pressures of the real world while delivering to them either a soul mate or an erotic lover in the form of a vampire. So, just what is the lure of the dead boyfriend to the modern female reader?

The Vampire as an Escape

In a world today filled with war and terrorism, many people look for ways to escape. The wives of the World War II era escaped their daily routines by reading romance novels and sharing them with their other married friends.

At the time, their heroes were soldiers, firemen, and police officers that would rescue the women from whatever danger they faced. They were the saviors of the young, weak female lead character.

In these stories, both male and female characters were written as physically perfect; however, it was the female that would have a helpless flaw or problem that only the lead character could fix. The hero would leave each day to do his "manly" job, come home to rescue her from whatever mess she would find herself in, and, at the end of the day, would please her in every way. These dreams were of what women would daydream and read.

But, today, the reader is no longer a dependent housewife that stays at home and cares for the family. As a result, fifty years later, this literature has developed in much the same way as the lead female character has developed.

She is now financially independent and lives alone. She is no longer the buxom blonde, but more of a girl-next-door type that the vampire finds so mysteriously alluring. She gets into trouble, but does not need rescuing. Instead, she assists in the adventure. She is her own hero that experiences this adventure equally with the vampire at her side. This is true of several series of vampire romance books, including the more popular Sookie Stackhouse Series by Charlaine Harris, Blood Series by Tanya Huff, Templar Vampires Series by Rene Lyons, and The Vampire Shrink Series by Linda Hilburn.

Author Linda Hilburn continued on her blog to discuss the question she is asked the most: "Why all the fuss about vampires?"

She found in her real-life private psychotherapy practice an upsurge in her women clients reporting that they dream of forbidden acts and romance with none other than the alluring vampire. She became fascinated with these dreams and began to question why they are occurring so often.

She found that, in today's world, women felt less secure than before, especially after the events of September 11, 2001. The once American heroes (police, soldiers, and firemen) were found to be destructible after that day. They suffered and died as heroes, but were not immortal.

What she came up with was that the modern female reader began to look for immortal and indestructible heroes. Their new chosen hero is the vampire, an aristocratic gentleman who can sweep you off your feet, romance you in ways you have never been romanced, and still survive an attack and live with you forever.

In her book, *The Vampire Shrink,* Hilburn tells the story of a young psychologist named Kismet Knight. She does not believe in the paranormal, but does want a little excitement in her life. She is bored with the life she leads and begins to look for something more, but is shocked by the dark supernatural world she finds.

This storyline is much like The Blood Series by Tanya Huff and her main female character, Vicki Nelson. Vicki is also a non-believer. She is a former police officer turned private investigator who has found herself in this dark world as well, with not only vampires, but witches and demons.

In both series, Kismet and Vicki are pulled into a love triangle between a human law enforcement officer and a vampire. Kismet's suitors are Alan Stevens, an FBI profiler and Devereux, an 800-year-old vampire. Vicki's suitors are former police partner Mike Celluci and Henry Fitzroy, the illegitimate vampire son of King Henry VIII.

These suitors attempt to protect and empower their female loves, but both the humans and the vampires offer something that the other cannot. The humans offer security, stability, and normality for the life that the female lead has always known. However, the vampire offers the "bad boy" appeal that most women have longed for at one time. They respect the female lead as a person, but at the same time, they want to protect and care for her.

This is the quandary that many women face today while trying to be both independent and feminine. They want to prove that they can do anything that they want to, but also let everyone know that just because they *can* do it all, it does not mean that they *have* to do it all.

The humans in these stories are still flawed, as are the real life men in the readers' world. Does anyone lust for an undead Al Bundy or does one crave that aristocrat that will provide for you, while at the same time empowering you to take the lead? Throughout these stories, vampires are not bound by human law and experience complete freedom. These bad boys are often flawed and need the female characters to help fix them, thus giving the female power over the male vampire.

Hilburn's clients expressed disappointment in the men in their real lives. They complained that they are ignored for football, beer, and television, and are overlooked in the bedroom. The real men in their lives take it for granted that they will always be there to take care of them. After living this life and reading these new vampire romance books, how many women are not going to open that window and let that mysterious stranger who is floating outside into their bedroom?

The Vampire as a Soul Mate

Many times in vampire literature, females are very accepting and nonjudgmental of who they love. They may be scared at certain times in the relationship, but are always looking for an equal in any relationship, no matter if he is a vampire. As a result, these female characters tend to be strong characters that are alive in the stories today.

These characters and their readers fall in love with these charismatic and seductive monsters. The vampire characters in the books display superhuman abilities. Vampires by nature can seduce the lead female character, defeat death, and physically destroy their enemies to protect. This is very seductive to the reader.

The vampire's superhuman abilities are coupled only with their struggle to hate the monster within. They hate who they are and what they have to do in order to survive. Many are doomed to walk the earth and to repent their sins from their previous life. During this internal struggle, these vampires tend to find their soul mate, that one woman who can deliver them from hell and love them all at the same time. This is the theme of The Templar Vampire Series by Rene Lyons.

In this story, there are five Templar Knights who fell from the grace of God by straying from his plan during the Crusades. Each of the five Templar Knights suffered a harsh childhood and an even more devastating adult life as a soldier for God. They murdered, raped, pillaged, and stole all in the name of religion but, as time went on, their mission strayed, as did their focus and commitment to God.

As it was in history, Rene wrote that King Philip IV of France charged the Templar Knights with heresy and had them executed. But, this is where the author's story changes history in this series of books.

Five of the knights – Constantine, Lucian, Tristan, Sebastian, and Raphael – were brought back from the dead by the archangel, Michael. Michael thrusts his spear and pulls their hearts from their chests. He declares that now they can only enter heaven once they find redemption in God's eyes for all of their sins. He declares them "undead" "vampire" "soulless" and tells them that in order to earn this redemption, they must find the Day Star and protect it until the time their redemption arrives.

In *Midnight Sun, Day Star, and Tempting Darkness*, the first three of the four that have been published, the Templar vampires struggle with the fact that they must find redemption and that, if one of them fails, then they all fail. Each book is the romantic adventure and story of each vampire and his chance at love and redemption. Each vampire struggles with who they were, who they have become, and the fear of damnation as each finds that "light in the darkness" that makes them stronger and allows them to find redemption.

Allison, Lexine, and Jessica are quiet girl-next-door types who may appear fragile, but have the strength and courage to help and to handle the love of the vampires: Sebastian, Constantine, and Lucian respectively. They follow the basic pattern of most vampire romance novels. They are a little fearful and cautious at first, they struggle together through the adventure while denying their love, then an explosive erotic love scene brings the meant-to-be soul mates together. The romance is the novel. The love is forever and the monster and female character are soul mates forever.

The Vampire as an Erotic Lover

Vampires have always been a metaphor for sex and taboo actions between a human and a monster. This monster is part of our deepest self that seduces us to let our dark side out and to allow the erotic to come through. Whether it was the great Victorian literature piece, *Dracula*, or the violently dark *Varney the Vampire: Feast of Blood*, the vampire is the one thing that we know we should not want, but can't live without – just one bite.

In *Dracula*, you read about the group sex between the three female vampires and Jonathan Harker, as well as the scene with Lucy, who is very promiscuous and juggles three male suitors. The scene where she is killed is very erotic and has been likened to gang rape. The image is simply three men taking a stake and penetrating her body violently and continuously.

But, the most erotic scene is when Mina is forced to drink Dracula's blood from his chest. It is a form of reverse breast feeding that shows Dracula not only as the provider of life, but the receiver of pleasure. At this time, the Count is an example of uncontrollable lust that is powerful, aggressive, and primal in nature. He is simply an example of parasitic love and a taboo of that time. However, today, the vampire bite and the sharing of blood represent eroticism, not violence. The vampire is seen as erotic, sensual, and oh so sexual.

In today's literature, the vampire has evolved to the perfect lover that can give the female everything she desires because they have had centuries of practice to give to only her and her alone. Vampires know what women need and take the time to please them.

For example, Sookie Stackhouse, the lead female character in the first book of The Sookie Stackhouse Series by Charlaine Harris is still a virgin because she is a telepath and can hear every thought that her human suitors have while they are trying to romance her. She finds this distracting and even disturbing, especially during make-out sessions. She says, "It's bad when you know that your date thinks your thighs are too fat." When she meets Bill Compton, the local vampire, she finds that she cannot read his mind and that she can finally relax and enjoy the company of a man, even though he is undead.

When her grandmother is killed, Bill begins to comfort her and they make love. The scene is one of complete attention and satisfaction of Sookie. She is the center of attention with every movement and action for her pleasure.

As time goes on, Sookie becomes a more active participant and even the one in control, at times offering her blood for his pleasure. This is the beginning of depicting women as at ease with their sexuality. But there is still the tie of emotion and of Bill being her first lover and vampire. In the real world, this is not always the case and this is what draws women to this genre.

But Charlaine does not stop there in this series. Sookie has a fall out with boyfriend Bill and has many suitors of all different species, including shifters, werewolves, and tigers. But the most erotic storyline is that of the hunky Viking Vampire, Eric Northman. He is hundreds of years old and is very careful of his and Sookie's relationship. He is not a fan of humans, but there is something unexplainable and strong that draws him to her. When they first meet, he asks Bill about her and Bill's response is, "She's mine." Bill shows his view of Sookie as property.

As the series goes on, the reader sees that Eric is beginning to view Sookie as an independent female that can take care of herself. Even though both vampires were alive during times in which women were seen as having to be cared for and rescued, Eric tries to modernize his thoughts on women without losing his status in the vampire world.

It is not until Eric loses his memory in *Dead to the World* that they consummate their relationship. Before this, Eric would portray both a business and physical interest in Sookie and would not give in to how deep his feelings were.

The scene between them was extremely erotic and empowering for Sookie. He gave her pleasure, but at the same time did not degrade or demoralize her. He allowed her to take control of the relationship, something he would have never done before the amnesia incident. He even offered to give up his position and power in the vampire world if that was what she wished. However, when he recovered, she did not tell him of the incident because she was unsure of how he would react if he knew that he had given himself to her mentally and physically. This strong sexual tension between the two continues to leave the reader waiting for more throughout the series, especially for the last installment that was released in May 2013. More about the uproar from the fans about the ending of the series will come later on in this book.

The vampire romance genre can range from mildly erotic to explicitly erotic. Women are not usually the consumers of film or print pornography because most usually are not visually stimulated. Women tend to lean towards written scenes to satisfy their real life desire. These vampire romance stories range from slight titillation to full-blown erotica, with no holds barred, blushing, and even "Oh my God" responses. If you were to Google "erotica vampire books" you would see over eight million websites listed. But, no matter the extent of the vampire book, the vampire is there to please the woman in whatever ways she wants.

Eroticism with a mixture of suspense is what has catapulted the Sookie Stackhouse series into the hit HBO Series, *True Blood.* This hit show, created by Alan Ball, has taken the eroticism to only the level that HBO can create – it has the most steamy sex scenes that have ever been produced by cable television. The popularity in this series shows that vampire literature is a genre with which to be reckoned. It has been announced that the series will end the summer of 2014.

Conclusion

Vampires are the new heroes of romance novels. They offer a soul mate concept with a lifetime of sexual experiences that is focused purely on the female. They offer escapism for the reader who is bored with her life as it is. For authors such as Tanya Huff, Rene Lyons, Charlaine Harris, and Lynda Hilburn, their vampires are invincible and here to help their readers through their day. They will continue to bring their vampires into our bedroom to please us in many ways. Devereaux, Bill, Eric, Henry, and Tristan will always be in the shadows of our dreams as well as forming our choices in our current mates or our search for one. Many readers wish for them to be floating outside their window and to have a chance to let them in, even if for just one night. This need for escapism will guarantee that vampire heroes are here to stay.

~ Did You Know?~

- Charlaine Harris received death threats because of how she ended the Sookie Stackhouse series? Fans were disappointed that Sookie didn't end up with vampires Eric or Bill, or were Alcide or even Quinn. Instead, she chose to end the story with Sookie ending with best friend and shifter Sam Merlotte. If fans had taken into account that Harris had said that Sookie would never become a vampire and that she wanted kids, then that would eliminate Eric and Bill. And Quinn had too much drama and she was never a fan of the mating rituals and laws for weres, so Sam was the obvious choice. He knew her secret and they could have kids. They could grow old together and be as normal as possible. Why is that so unbelievable?

- After Melissa de la Cruz ended her Blue Blood Series in December 2013, she decided that she would do a spin-off series that would bring about a new cycle of old and new vampires. Vampires of Manhattan: The New Blue Bloods Coven will be released in September of 2104. In between series, the author has been successful with other projects, such as a television show based on her other series, Witches of East End.

- Elizabeth Loraine, author of the Royal Blood Chronicle Series branched out from teen vampires to a more adult romantic title Corporate Ties. It is a little more risqué than her young adult series. Check it out on Amazon.

~~Reviews of Vampire Books~~

~Review of *The Vampire Sonnets* by David Bradsher~

The Vampire Sonnets by David Nelson Bradsher is the most passionate and unique vampire book that has been published in modern times.

It tells the story of Tristan Grey, a 19th Century Londoner, who is seduced and turned by Lady Nina, leader of the Chelsea Clan. But things aren't always what they seem through the eyes of a fledgling immortal. What sets this project apart from the countless other vampire tales in the marketplace currently is that these are written in sequential Shakespearean sonnets

Despite any preconceived notions that readers may have about a book of sonnets being boring and dry, Bradsher pulled off one of the most unique stories ever.

Once the pattern of the iambic pentameter begins in your head, the rhythm in his words will match the street fighting, the biting, and the loving that is occurring in the story.

The descriptions in the book of London were very accurate. The dampness of the alleys, the crispness of the air, the desperation, and the passion of the characters are all there for the reader to actually envision.

The most viscous vampire in the story is Tristan's sire, Nina. The role of women in this sonnet written by a man is intriguing. Each female, whether it is Nina, Maggie, or Supriya, shows women as independent females that take charge of their lives and the choices that they make, whether good or bad. It is their choice to make and no one else's.

Also, the concept of them being described by Nina as a succubus is romantic, yet so deadly. The passion, the love, and the hate in this sonnet adds to the action and mystery that makes this book perfect for any reader whether it be a Shakespearean expert, a student, or a lover of vampire stories such as me.

The Vampire Sonnets is a highly recommended book for any vampire lover. It is a wonderful and unique story to add to that vampire literature collection. David has found a way to bring nobility and grace back to the vampire while bringing them to the present. It may be found at www.nelsonpearlpublishers.com

~Review of *The Vampire Shrink* by Lynda Hilburn~

The Vampire Shrink by Lynda Hilburn has recently been released with a new publisher and a fresh rewrite. The book is the first in the *Knight the Vampire Psychologist Series.*

Kismet Knight is a psychologist who lives in Denver, Colorado. She has lived the basic life of a strong, independent female professional. She has had a few unsuccessful relationships and, as most professional women, has been "focusing" on her career rather than on herself or her career.

One day, a young Goth vampire wannabe teen named Midnight comes into Dr. Knight's office and begins to introduce her to the world of the vampire. She is thrown into a world that most mortals never know about or want to know.

Because of a police investigation, she meets FBI profiler, Alan Stephens, as well as 800-year-old vampire Devereux. She is torn between both worlds as well as her feelings for each.

This book is full of adventure, romance, and humor. Mrs. Hilburn addresses everyday items while making her world connect to ours. Kismet Knight is a wonderful professional female character that is very independent and tough while maintaining her femininity. This book only begins to tempt our taste buds for more stories of the Denver Vampire Shrink.

It is refreshing to have a literary character that embodies and symbolizes intelligence and independence over looks and sex appeal. Kismet shows that even smart professional women can have a good time. There is just the perfect mix of romance, mysticism, mystery, and humor to make this a joyful read.

The second in the Knight the Vampire Psychologist series is *Blood Therapy* and was released in 2013 and the third installment *Crimson Psyche* was released in the UK in January of 2014, but no word yet of the US release date.

Lynda Hilburn also has other novellas available for the vampire lovers:

- *Until Death Do Us Part*

- *Devereux: The Night Before Kismet*

- *Diary of a Narcissistic Bloodsucker*

- *Undead in the City*

- *Sex in a Coffin*

You can find out more about Lynda and her books on her website at: http://paranormalityuniverse.blogspot.com

~Review of *Relations that Suck: The Story of Eva and Dries* by Marilyn Yu~

Relations that Suck: The Story of Eva and Dries by Marilyn Yu is more than just a spellbinding, emotional story, but also a visionary delicacy for your senses.

The story itself is one to which any reader can relate. The characters struggle with who they are, with the consequences of their actions and with their finding a relationship between each other that extends further than either would believe.

Eva is a vampire who struggles with who she is. She has adapted to feeding only as needed and as little as she needs to survive. Dries is a spider that cannot handle the mundane world of web spinning and searches for a new meaning to his life. They meet and share a relationship that is life changing. The author weaves a story that makes you yearn to know more.

But the amazement of the story is not all that Ms. Yu has contributed to this book. She is also credited with the Art Director, Clothing Designer, and Artist title. Each page of the book is a photograph of different models as they go through the struggle of the story. The pictures are so inviting that you find yourself inside each page. The details of the symbols, the clothing, and even the doilies are so exquisite that one can stare at each page and wonder what profound meaning each holds.

The author knows that her beautifully dressed vampire and large spider will make her readers want to know more and she provides this on her website. Yu provides us with a free study guide on her website as well. This study guide tells the meaning of each character, picture, and symbol located within the book.

Ms. Yu wrote that she may write a prequel telling of Eva's life before she met Dries. I encourage her to do this and will be one of the first in line to buy the book. Ms. Yu is a talented artist in both visual and literary talents and has created a piece of art that tempts all of the readers' senses. It is definitely a book to be collected and enjoyed.

Relations That Suck and Marilyn's second book, *LaFemme Fatale* (that is a book that is made into huge tarot cards) may be found on Marilyn's website at www.marilynyu.com.

~Review of The Brookhaven Vampires by Joann I. Martin Sowles ~

Joann I. Martin Sowles, author of The Brookhaven Vampire Series, has brought to young adult and adult readers one of the most refreshing vampire books in a long time.

Laney is the first book in the series and the main character, Laney, is a wonderful representation of what it would be like to today's world if a nineteen-year-old met a cute boy in class and he happened to be a vampire, or at least in our dreams. The setting is in the real world, a small college campus, and the events that take place are easily ones that readers can picture themselves in. This is unlike many stories where the girl whines about the boy; yes there is teen angst. It is a young adult book, after all, but it really brings about the strength that makes who she becomes in the future books.

Darkness is the second book in the series and picks up after the crazy war between brothers, vampires, and werewolves that ended Book Two. *Darkness* takes us deeper into that world. The battle is over and Carter, who has vampire lineage, has been bitten by a werewolf and this mixture has never been seen in this world. Is he in danger? Will he survive? Carter is one of my favorite characters in this book especially the "Chicken Suit" chapter.

Laney spends most of her time at Julz House in this story. She ventures out some, but this is the only thing I felt either could have sped up the story or slowed it down. The reader begins to learn more about the history of the vampires here and it is truly something.

Tainted Blood is the third book in the series and it focuses on the relationship between Laney and Oliver. The second half of the book allows Laney to grow on her own and begin to learn more about the people she calls friends, the history behind Brookhaven, and, even more importantly, herself. The best part of the book is when they begin attending night class and learn more about paranormal studies.

Zane, the Guardian Angel is a novella that came out between *Tainted Blood* and the next book, *Cursed.* Zane fell to earth when Laney turned nineteen. He is her protector, but there is more to Zane than we know in *Tainted Blood* and, in this novella, we learn Zane's back story and how he came to be on earth.

The final book at this time is *Cursed*. The previous books were labeled as young adult and this one is labeled as adult contemporary/young adult, not for anyone younger than eighteen. So, this tells the reader there is much more blood, violence, and sex than in the previous books. This book really is what the reader has been wanting – answers to characters' identities, histories, and futures.

This series mixes the right amount of action and romance that will hold any reader to the story. This is one of the best young adult series that one could choose to read.

For more information on Joann I. Martin Sowles and her Brookhaven Vampires, check out her website here: http://www.brookehavenvampires.com/

~Interviews with Vampire Authors~

In this edition, I have added several interviews of authors that I think represent a great mixture of the vampire genre – romance, historical, young adult, erotic, and traditional vampires. I hope that you enjoy these interviews and please feel free to contact these authors. They are very approachable.

~Interview with Nathan Squires, author of the Crimson Shadow Series~

Question: Tell me about yourself and why you wanted to write books about vampires.

Answer: I suppose a great deal of my pull towards vampires and telling their stories stems from a childhood fear of them. Their mystery and power and ability to lurk undetected until the last moment in darkness made for many nights where I'd lay awake and stare into the corner of my room expectantly, and it's quite possible that the sleep deprivation as a child resulted in some developmental disruption. As I got older, my fear gave way to an obsession and, as an interest in writing grew, the two met and became quickly comfortable as a pair in my stories.

I see vampires and creatures like them as a fascinating and intriguing way to add dramatic and enticing depths to a story while, at the same time, maintaining the element of a human psychosis. Stories of space aliens or dragons or other such creatures involve a very dramatic separation from the human element, and, while I enjoy a super-powered fight between paranormal creatures and excessive bloodshed, there's a foundation of something relatable that a reader can SEE in being a vampire or werewolf or what-have-you that they can't have for a winged quadruped or off-green drone that dropped from a saucer.

Question: What series do you write? Please describe it in one to two paragraphs.

Answer: I am the author of the Crimson Shadow series, which centers on the young Xander Stryker and follows his descent from being a tortured and suicidal teen into the grips of a vampiric cult that has ties to his late father. Deciding to abandon his human life in an effort to seek a sense of belonging in a world he's unknowingly always been a part of, he starts down a path of self-realization and reinvention.

The series begins with Xander discovering and combatting with his agonizing history while, at the same time, trying to survive his own self-destructive tendencies and unbridled rage. Each novel of the seven-book series will bring Xander closer to realizing the legacy he was destined to reach as well as closer to the brink of his own strained sanity.

Question: Are your characters based off of any vampires in pop culture?

Answer: *Tilts hand back and forth* Yes/no…

I think the visual aspects and certain quirks to the characters' personalities may have fragments of popular vampire characters, but I tend to shy away from incorporating preexisting characters from other sources as inspiration. For the most part, I try to build my characters off of a "skeleton" that might be a person/celebrity or personality-type that I feel appropriately defines what I need and build over that with aesthetic traits and styles. Because, in many ways, other pop-culture vampires are based on an exaggerated reference from that author's mind, my using THEIR work to define my own would be an exaggeration of an exaggeration, and I can't help but see that as similar to Xeroxing an already copied document (eventually you begin to sacrifice quality and depth).

Question: Are your books based off of any stories in pop culture?

Answer: No. All of my work is based on situational circumstances. I make characters and build enough personality so that, when I stick them in whatever plot-line I've developed, their character "pilots" the course of the story. I prefer to work from a psychological angle than try to metaphorically play off of something directly.

It's been said that there's only a few ORIGINAL story-lines (less than a dozen, if I remember correctly) and that, in some way, all stories fall into one of those "patterns." Because of this, nothing – no matter how much one tries – can ever TRULY be "original," so I accept that somewhere out there is something that parallels my own work and, no doubt, there will be future works that parallel my own. That being said, I accept that I've probably inadvertently followed some pre-existing story, but it certainly was never my intent to do so.

Question: Who is your favorite vampire?

Answer: I can't say that I have a FAVORITE vampire, *per se*. Like movies and music and literature, a lot of what motivates a "favorite" is determined by mood and current interests. If I'm in the middle of an anime-craze, then my favorite vampire would probably be Alucard from Hellsing (yes, as the name suggests his lineage is hinted towards THE Dracula, but a lot of the more noted similarities are blurred by large-caliber handguns and visually-dramatic and excessively gory sequences [if such a thing is truly possible]). I'd have to say one of my favorite horror movie vampires would be Collin Ferrell's depiction of the vampire, Jerry, in the 2011 remake of *Fright Night* (the movie as a whole wasn't a personal favorite, but Ferrell's subtle nuances as an ancient vampire – little twitches or gestures that gave a new dimension to the role – made me want to see more of him and less of everybody else). As a fan of music (and the heavier stuff, at that), if I get into a particularly jam-packed mood, I tend to lean more towards Aaliya and Stuart Townsend as Queen Akasha and Lestat from *Queen of the Damned* (I personally feel drawn towards vampires that balance terror and beauty, and I don't think I'm alone when I say that *Queen of the Damned* had that in abundance). In literature, because of my adoration of cinematic action and gnarly fights, I lean towards vampires like Sonja Blue from Nancy A. Collins' Sunglasses after Dark series.

To be honest (if not a tad predictable and self-absorbed), I'd say that my FAVORITE vampire is Xander Stryker from my Crimson Shadow series. However, in my defense, I shaped the character from a lot of the aforementioned traits along with some personality traits that I, personally, felt were lacking in the vampire spectrum.

Question: What are your favorite books to read?

Answer: My favorite books are the ones that balance healthy doses of the supernatural/paranormal/occult with deeper, more profound subject matter. I love my books to have an inherent layer of raw entertainment value as well as a complex and relevant message to deliver. A lot of the best books for me are the ones that bring the protagonist's psychosis into play (call me deranged, but tortured/warped characters that have to fight as much with themselves as the external antagonist are more compelling). Most of the time, this lands me in more gritty fantasy or horror.

Question: If you use mythology in your books, what is it, why did you use it, and can you tell me in about a paragraph or two about this myth?

Answer: The mythology in the Crimson Shadow series (and all of my work, for that matter – yes, it's all the same "world") is a custom-tailored world set in the here-and-now with a list of creatures that have been tweaked/altered from a slew of myths around the world. When I decided to become serious about my writing, I wanted a world – and a community of non-human creatures (known as "mythos") – that were both recognizable and believable while, at the same time, were fresh and mysterious. Because EVERYBODY'S seen or read of the popular legends, to try and create a world that would shock and amaze the main character as he delved deeper into their existence, I needed to make something that was equally as shocking and amazing to the readers that would be journeying beside him. A lot of this involved taking concepts of evolution and biology into account when I tried to get into a lot of the "how" and "why" of things.

In the end, I ended up creating a world with over four subspecies of vampire (blood-drinkers known as "sangsuigas"/"sangs" that have various "levels" of being based on how they became vampires (born, made, or bitten BY a "made"), psychic vampires that rely on their auras as invisible appendages to fight and feed called "aurics," another species that is comprised of the two – basically what the original vampires started as before evolution split the feeding methods for one reason or another – called "perfects," and another vampiric species that has not yet been touched down on, but are, for lack of a better word, "gods/goddesses" of the mythos world.

Also, because I feel that a paranormal world should be as diverse as any other sort of community, I altered the werewolf legends to not strictly center on wolves, but ALL animals. Because people aren't shaped or colored the same way, I saw no reason for them all to look the same in another form. For this reason, some of these creatures – which I refer to as "theriomorphs" (or "therions" for short, "therio-" being a Latin root for "beast") – will have a more wolf/canine-like appearance while others may be more cat-like and others may appear more like bears or primates, based on their build in their human bodies.

While there's a great many other creatures in the series, the above examples are a prime example of the sorts of alterations I've made to the popular legends. In the end, I wanted something that was believable and new while not obliterating or overly-warping the creatures we've all grown up loving.

Question: What do you see in your future for your series?

Answer: Love. Loss. Growth. Pain. Revelations. Death. Victories.

And lots and lots of bloody battles.

To tell the truth, I never expected to see the project that was the first book go THIS far. When I wrote it, I was suicidal and trying to get down on paper what I felt/saw in my mind as a sense of closure before I took my own life. Crimson Shadow started off as a creative suicide letter and, halfway through, became a life-saving project. Trying to have Xander find a way to survive his own desires to die passed on to me, and I found myself wanting to tell more of his story in the hopes that he could potentially inspire others to choose life as well. Since then, I've had a few people come to me and confess that *Crimson Shadow: Noir* (book #1) WAS an inspiration and that they've since found a new reason to live (it's also why my publisher and I decided to donate a portion of the book's proceeds to the anti-suicide/self-harm group, TWLOHA).

At this point, knowing that I've both entertained AND saved lives with my work, I don't really aspire for anything else. I'll continue to write and hope that it continues to do what it's doing, and I certainly won't complain about any advancement, but at this point, I think it would just be extra frosting on the cake.

Question: What makes your series unique?

Answer: I suppose a lot of what separates Crimson Shadow from other series is the brutal reality of the content. Sure, the series is set in a paranormal world of vampires and monsters, but so often, in an effort to be "supernatural scary," authors forget just how messed-up the REAL world can be. There are real terrors existing in this world, and it doesn't take a work of fiction to reveal true monsters. Xander's tortured upbringing is due to an event from his childhood in which his abusive stepfather and a group of men assault and murder his mother that took place in front of him. Subject matter like murder, rape, suicide, and torture/bullying have rapidly been swept away as a social taboo that people think will disappear just by ignoring it. I feel that this is a disservice to people who have suffered these such atrocities, because, just like the acts are cast away like some sort of horrible rumor, those that suffer from them are shunned and looked down on SIMPLY because their existence means little more to the masses than evidence that what they wish was fiction DOES exist. For me, to put these truths in the spotlight as the abominable acts that they are--to dangle them in the faces of any who would try to ignore them-- and say "You SEE what this does to people? You SEE what simply looking away achieves?" I feel that if people want these things to stop, then the only proper response is to fight it, and you can't fight an enemy that you refuse to face.

I also feel that the world and the creatures that occupy it do a great job of illustrating a balance between the humanity in monsters and the monsters in humanity as well as taking a great deal of psychological and philosophical approaches to the genre.

Beyond this, as a film/anime and comic/manga enthusiast, I feel that my approach to paranormal fight sequences and more visually-dynamic scenes takes on a very "cinematic" effect (a term that I've seen used in a few reviews lately) that validates a great deal of my efforts to write a book that people can "see."

Question: What are your favorite things about vampires in pop culture today?

Answer: I think a lot of my fascination and intrigue with vampires in modern media is how infinite the spectrum has become. I'm certainly not the first author to make alterations, and throughout the decades of bending and warping and tweaking, we're blessed with a range of vampire that spans from the hideously wretched and murderous to obscenely beautiful and generous. All shapes, sizes, forms, functions, and possibilities exist, and more continue to be developed each and every year! I honestly cannot think of a single other legend that has such a broad and varied range of potential, and the beauty of this is that there is, in some form or another, a breed of vampire for ANY sort of person!

Romance, horror, sci-fi, western, historical, musical, action, children, YA, comics, erotica, detective, occult... there is no genre that the beloved life-feeders CAN'T comfortably fit in through their sheer diversity! For me, as somebody whose job it is to use vampires to ENTERTAIN, this range allows for an all-too-rare freedom in how to approach a project and optimize my target audience's enjoyment of the piece.

Question: What is your least favorite things about vampires in pop culture today?

Answer: Some people misuse the aforementioned freedom and create something so far out of the vampire realm that many have a hard time following the stories.

Question: Where can we find you on the internet?

Answer: I'm actually on over fifty-five networking sites of some sort or another, so finding me is never really a challenge, but if you visit my author site at www.nathansquiers.com you'll be able to explore my work, formally join The Legion (I don't like the word "fans"– I find it condescending and disrespectful and feel that it strips individuals of their identity as supporters – and, instead, have people in The Legion who follow my work), personally contact me, as well as find links to my Facebook, Twitter, and other such pages. Both my work and I can be found on Amazon.

~Interview with Sarah Glenn, author of *All This and Family, Too*~

Question: Tell me about yourself and why you wanted to write books about vampires.

Answer: I was born a strange child who matured into an odd grownup. Somewhere in between, I ran a vampire game in which my wife played Cynthia. This proves two things: Cynthia is not my Mary Sue, since she is not an idealized version of myself, and some muses are Irish rather than Greek.

I wrote Cynthia because I loved Gwen's character and the situations we created together. Does that mean I'm writing fan fiction?

Question: What series do you write?

Answer: I tell the tale of Cynthia Leach, a gifted astronomer who can no longer teach daytime classes due to her disability: "adult-onset porphyria." All she wants to do is lead a normal unlife. In my first novel, she moves her family members into a gated community to protect them from vampire hunters – only to learn that the Homeowners' Association is much harder to deal with. The term "Deed Restriction" takes on a whole new meaning for her.

Question: Are your characters based off of any vampires in pop culture?

Answer: My "regular" vampires have the powers that Dracula displayed in the Hammer films, but their conflicts are more practical than archetypal.

Question: Are your books based off of any stories in pop culture?

Answer: Um. No, not really. I did try watching The Gates to see if it was anything like my work, but it wasn't even close. It also wasn't very interesting, which I hope is not the case with my novel.

Question: What do you see in your future for your series?

Answer: Assuming I don't slash my wrists before the sequel is finished... Cynthia will continue her struggle for a normal unlife. Unfortunately, vampires are not normal, and they don't attract normal problems into their unlives. Cynthia set some things into motion at the end of the first novel, and they're going to bite her in the ass.

Question: What makes your series unique?

Answer: One person told me that he thought I'd told the story of a handicapped person – it just happened to be vampirism in her case. What I really enjoy writing, though, is the family dynamic. There are no hierarchies of bloodlines, just Grandma, Cynthia, her brother, and the people they adopt as time goes on.

Question: Who is your favorite vampire?

Answer: Barnabas Collins, as played by Jonathan Frid (although Johnny Depp's remake is closer to the type of story I write). After that, it would be a tie between George Hamilton in *Love at First Bite* and Grandpa from *The Munsters*.

Question: What are your favorite books to read?

Answer: I love medical thrillers, followed by psychological thrillers. I like very, very dark stuff that happens to human beings. When I get tired of drama, I enjoy Carl Hiaasen.

Question: If you use mythology in your books, what is it, why did you use it, and can you tell me in about a paragraph or two about this myth?

Answer: For my short story, "Caldera of Trouble," I did serious research on the vrykolakas – aka the Greek Vampire. The vampires in my novel, *All This and Family, Too* are based on the "traditional" movie vampire, minus the castle and plus a lot of bureaucratic complication.

Many authors create vampires that are descendants of gods, angels, or aliens, but I rarely enjoy reading about them. To me, those are stories about gods, angels, or aliens that drink blood – not "real" vampires.

Question: What is your favorite thing about vampires in pop culture today?

Answer: Due to the boost in popularity, the market for "nontraditional" and funny vampire stories has opened up. The Undead and Unwed series by Mary Janice Davidson and *You Suck: a Love Story* by Christopher Moore are good examples.

Question: What are your least favorite things about vampires in pop culture today?

Answer: Too. Many. Of. Them. Vampires lose the "cool" factor if they're in every supermarket. Fortunately, they are being replaced by zombies. There's probably some sort of unpleasant cultural shift driving this changeover, but vampires are immortal and will always be with us.

Question: Where can we find you on the internet?

Answer: I can be found at my website here www.sarahglenn.com

~Interview with S.P. Hendrick, author of the Tales of the Dearg-Sidhe Series~

Question: Tell me about yourself and why you wanted to write books about vampires.

Answer: I am an avid reader. When the kids my age were reading comic books, I had devoured all the library had on world mythology and had branched out into reading Robert Heinlein and Andre Norton and all the science fiction and fantasy I could get my hands on, which was the modern world's version of mythology. I have thirty-four overflowing bookcases and am looking for more room to set up another one.

I never expected to write a vampire novel, let alone a series. *Dubhghall* just sort of happened one hot and blazing afternoon at a Renaissance Faire when I saw a very interesting young man in full kilt and fangs and realized there had to be a story...so I went home and let the character tell one. Is he a vampire? Not the typical type. He is the son of Ireland's greatest hero, Cuchulainn, made immortal by the Battle Goddess Morrigan, who must drink human blood. He is immune to sunlight because his grandfather is Lugh, a Celtic solar deity. He is also immune to any natural element, but he has enemies, powerful enemies, whom he fights over millennia.

He also cannot make another like himself. He is alone. He is a Dearg-Sidhe, which my British publisher translates as "Blood-Faery."

Question: What series do you write? Please describe it in one to two paragraphs?

Answer: Tales of the Dearg-Sidhe, beginning in the early First Century CE, tracks the adventures of Dubhghall mac Cu, eldest son of Cuchulainn, given immortality by the Irish Goddess Morrigan in exchange for his duty to watch over Her people throughout history until the Sidhe return to Tara Mound. He fights against the Romans, the Normans, and all else who would lay false claim to the British Isles, including an evil far older than they who would send the Shining Ones and the people They protect into the darkness of annihilation.

Question: What do you see in your future for your series?

Answer: I am working through British history right now. Whenever I see dots to connect, I do so and come up with pictures historians would probably never see. I am working on one in the Elizabethan era and one in the Victorian era, and am trying to decide whether Richard III deserves a whole book or if he will just be a flashback in the Elizabethan book. After that he will probably make a few modern and future appearances before he ends up off-planet in The Blood of Kings in the other series in the far future. He does appear in the background throughout that series, but not as a major character. I am also working on a third companion series, The Glastonbury Archives, which gives a lot of background to the other two and tell stories of other characters involved in both of them, and there is a Tarot card set in the works.

Question: What makes your series unique?

Answer: A combination of history, mythology, folklore, and Pagan motifs, which link together a hero who just happens to be immortal and needs to live on the blood of humans.

Question: Who is your favorite vampire?

Answer: When I was growing up, there was really only one vampire, unless one counted Nosferatu, and that was Dracula. Whether it was Bela Lugosi or Christopher Lee, it was still The Count. Later on, there were choices, and I would have to say of them I loved Nick Knight in the old TV series *Forever Knight* and Angel of *Buffy the Vampire Slayer* and *Angel*, both of whom had socially redeeming qualities. I was fascinated by Lestat at first, but his selfishness often wanted to make me throw the books across the room.

Question: What are your favorite books to read?

Answer: Right now, British history, as I am researching a lot of things for the Tales of the Dearg-Sidhe series and the companion Glastonbury Chronicles series. When I have time to read for pleasure, it is usually fantasy and science fiction or mystery as well as the classics and any new insights I can get on mythology.

Question: If you use mythology in your books, what is it, why did you use it, and can you tell me in about a paragraph or two about this myth?

Answer: I tend to use Celtic mythology, mostly Irish and Scottish with the story of Cuchulainn in *Son of Air and Darkness*, with a bit of Roman also as I have Dubhghall fighting with Boudicca against the Romans, broadening it into some Cornish in *The Great Queen's Hound*, and even bringing in a touch of British folklore with Robin Hood in *The Pale Mare's Fosterling*. By the time Dubhghall makes an appearance as a major character in Volume V of The Glastonbury Chronicles, The Blood of Kings, and the forthcoming Volume VI *The Barley and the Rose*, I bring in Welsh mythology as well.

There are two underlying myths: Cuchulainn was given Uathach, the daughter of his teacher Scathach, as his bride. That is about the last time she is mentioned in mythology, for he soon took up with Aoife and had by her a son named Connlai, whom he later killed in battle. But what if Connlai had a half-brother by Uathach, Dubhghall, who was claimed by The Morrigan to watch with her till the Sidhe returned to Tara Mound? The other myth is that of the Sacred King, a king whose blood must be shed to make fertile the land and save its people. And what if the guardian of the King who dies as a willing sacrifice is guarded by an immortal creature that lives on blood but may not touch the blood of the King?

Question: What is your favorite thing about vampires in pop culture today?

Answer: They have such wonderful wardrobes.

Question: What is your least favorite thing about vampires in pop culture today?

Answer: They are becoming stereotypes and two dimensional.

Question: Where can we find you on the internet?

Answer: www.SPHendrick.com .

~Interview with BittenTwice, author of the Macedo Ink Series~

Question: Tell me about yourself and why you wanted to write books about vampires?

Answer: Hi, my name is BittenTwice. I hide behind my name like a vampire, thriving off of anonymity while drifting through the ages. The boring detail might say I'm a mother of two, living in sunny south Florida. It's the best place to hide. Only a few look for vampires hiding close to the equator. The fun details all unfold after the sun goes down.

Question: What series do you write? Please describe it in one to two paragraphs?

Answer: I write the Macedo Ink series:

Alexander, 2000-year-old vampire once known as Alexander the Great, lives in New York City masquerading as Lex Macedo, web-hosting billionaire. His lovely wife is none other than Catalina De Diablo, Princess of Abaddon and Lucifer's crowned heir to the underworld. Alex has also been tasked with protecting the Peace Keeper as her Dark Warrior, accompanied by Michael the Archangel as Light's Warrior. Together, they fight to maintain the balance between heaven and hell and more often between light and dark, wherever that occurs. From vampires gone rogue to imprisonment in a human jail compounded by stints made to heaven and hell, life is never without challenges in Alex's world. He also battles with an emotion he has never had to face – love. In both his natural and unnatural lives, he has never had to worry about the emotions unveiled by being in love and loving the devil's daughter has challenges. From possession to blood sucking haute couture fashion, and demonic fetish, Alex finds that loving Lina requires more than just time.

Question: Are your characters based off of any vampires in pop culture?

Answer: My vampires definitely are more in line with the European representation. Some of the cultural vampires have a few unattractive features such as the peeling of skin, and fire from their armpits that wouldn't work well, though I've been introducing them into the storyline. I can see shared traits, like the broodiness exhibited by the Salvatore brothers (*Vampire Diaries*), the craving for normal seen in Henry Fitzroy (*Blood Ties*), and the flare for adventure seen in Carlos Rivera (Vampire Huntress Series)

Question: Are your books based off of any stories in pop culture?

Answer: There's no one book that mine are based off of. Though I will say that once an author defines the vampire, then we all share some similar traits to each other.

Question: What do you see in your future for your series?

Answer: I have thirteen titles lined up for the series so far and, after that, who knows where the story will go.

Question: What makes your series unique?

Answer: My characters. They shake their fists at the societal norm; after all, they do live in the paranormal. Girl meets hunk of a vampire and lives for a few years after does not excite me. I want the hunger, the thirst, the visceral nature of my characters to show, tempered perhaps only by inappropriate compassion, question, and the root of both good and evil – Love.

Question: Who is your favorite vampire?

Answer: Only one? I really liked Henry Fitzroy from Tanya Huff's books, he was so conflicted, but then again, I love the broody visceral Eric Northman from True Blood, though on the other hand, the lone wolf Blade stands out as a force to be reckoned with.

Question: What are your favorite books to read?

Answer: I like dark fantasy sprinkled with adventure. Take me somewhere and show me something... something that will appease my mind as well as my heart.

Question: If you use mythology in your books, what is it, why did you use it, and can you tell me in about a paragraph or two about this myth?

Answer: Greek mythology is interlaced throughout my Macedo Ink series, along with the bindings of Christianity. We all see with our eyes, but sometimes, when we look at a puzzle piece, we come away with one story that is such a minuscule part of the big picture that the story only provides misdirection. My main character is a two-thousand-year-old vampire who, in real life, was Alexander the Great. The gods that he knew as a child are still watching, as is the God of today. Meshing old with new makes for fun interactions and often provides the foundation for chaos or the key for resolution.

Question: What are your favorite things about vampires in pop culture today?

Answer: They are so mainstream. They could be anyone or anywhere. Would you know? Next time you are people-watching, see if you can pick them out of the crowd.

Question: What are your least favorite things about vampires in pop culture today?

Answer: They are so mainstream. Authors can manipulate them into molds and, like an outlier on a statistical graph, they become a potential for a new norm.

Question: Where can we find you on the internet?

Answer: www.bitten2ice.com

~Interview with Laura Enright, author of *Vampires Most Wanted: The 10 Bloodthirsty Biters and other Undead Oddities*~

Question: Tell me about yourself and why you wanted to write books about vampires.

Answer: I wrote my book, *Vampires' Most Wanted: The Top 10 Book of Bloodthirsty Biters, Stake-wielding Slayers, and Other Undead Oddities*, curiously enough, for the sake of my other vampires. I'd been trying to find a home for a vampire series set in Chicago that I'd written. I was approached by Potomac Publishing, the publisher that puts out the Most

Wanted series, to write a follow up to my 2004 *Chicago's Most Wanted* book. The topic we originally considered fell through, so I suggested that I do a *Most Wanted* book on vampires. Not only is the topic interesting, but I hoped it would give me a little boost with finding a home for my vampire fiction series. I was astounded by how much was out there regarding vampires, what with literature, TV, movies, legends. It's a fascinating topic on a number of levels.

As for my vampire series, I had an idea rolling around in my head for the character of Narain Khan. I sort of challenged myself to see if I could write the story and *To Touch the Sun* blossomed from there and I fell in love with the characters. I've since finished four novels in the series, working title The Khan Family Series, and a spinoff novel using two ghost hunter characters that appear in novel number three. I can't stop telling these stories. It's become a bit of an obsession. And I think one of the most fascinating things for me with any vampire fiction is the back story. So many tales can be mined from the back story. Writing these novels has been a treat.

Question: What series do you write? Please describe it in one or two paragraphs.

Answer: The first book is titled *To Touch the Sun*. The main story is set in present-day Chicago, but has flashbacks to World War I when a young Indian named Narain Khan left his native India to fight in France. It was his hope to stay on after the war and learn the art of European cooking, which was his passion, but during a push through No Man's Land, he was wounded and was left for dead, then was attacked by wild vampires that roamed the battlefields, looking for victims. He became a sentient vampire and, with the help of the Frenchman Alphonse (who lost his son to wild vampires), he began to believe that he could live as normal a life as possible with the peculiarities of the condition. Eventually, he met a woman named Sophie who became his wife and his food source and helped him navigate the decades after his conversion.

When the novel opens, Sophie has been dead a year and the blood stored up is gone. Narain, now a popular chef and restaurateur in Chicago, finds himself in the position of needing to hunt to find food, something he finds morally repulsive that he hasn't had to do for a very long time, but is something he must eventually attend to because, at some point, his body will give him no choice and he might not be able to control the act. Complicating matters is that two ghosts from his past have come to town. Reginald Jameson was a sadistic bully when he was a captain in the trenches and, as a vampire, is even more dangerous. Fred Blythe, a friend of Narain's from the trenches and now a vampire also, had been captured by Jameson a few years before in an attempt to discover the secret behind the half-mad vampire's ability to walk in the sun. The experiments conducted in Jameson's lab have created a crazed mutant vampire named Boris, who Blythe has come to Chicago to destroy. On top of all this, Narain has fallen in love with Cassie Lambert, a woman he meets at a fundraiser. His business partner Dom, a normal human, suggests that he pursue her, but as Narain says, his condition isn't something easily explained over a romantic dinner, which he couldn't eat anyway. Yet, as it turns out, Cassie may know more about Narain than he ever suspects.

Question: Are your characters based off any vampires in pop culture?

Answer: Not really. I tried to go against type (the ultra-cool, melancholic, slightly ethereal vampire). I liked the idea of making the lead character a non-European vampire, and someone whose vampire skills are a bit rusty because he's been out of practice. Actually, the character itself was inspired by a character that the Indian actor Shah Rukh Khan played in the Bollywood film Main Hoon Na. He plays a character that is sort of forced to go out of his element to try to save lives. And that sort of idea of leaving the comfort of what you know to do the right thing struck me. Narain as a vampire has had it rather lucky for decades having Sophie as his food source. He's grown complacent and her death has sort of forced him back into a situation that he didn't feel comfortable with. Now he has to figure out how to deal with the realities of his condition, while keeping the life he's created intact in the face of a number of other crises going on around him. It's fun to throw things into the mix that knock him off balance. As Reg says in the second novel, "I don't envy you your life, Khan. It always seems that you're placed in situations where, no matter what choice you make, you stand to lose something."

Question: Are your books based off of any stories in pop culture?

Answer: No, not stories, *per se*. Concepts, maybe. For example, I write the vampirism as a medical condition, which is something that has been done for a while (I think Matheson was one of the first). I do use some of the beliefs (like the harmful effects of sunlight. The notion that vampires are stronger than normal people and live eternally). Like Matheson, I try to explain these things medically. Like I mentioned, I wanted to play against type a bit. I also wanted to play around with the idea of a vampire that didn't have it very easy, as has been the case with one of the vampire characters that first appears in the second novel of the series. He's a vampire whose fortunes rise and fall over the many years of his life and part of the battle is retaining his sense of morality during the downtimes when it's not quite as easy. He's slept in suites and had to bunk out in used graves, depending on his fortunes. As he says, "Not all vampires have castles in Transylvania."

Question: What do you see in the future for your series?

Answer: Hopefully, a lot of success. I think it's a fun series. It's been fun not only to write current plots, but also the back stories of these characters that appear in the novels (in fact, the third novel is primarily about the life of the hard luck vampire during a year in the 1930s). What were they like before they became vampires? How did they become vampires? How did that affect who they were? How do they get along in society? I find those questions to be some of the more fascinating aspects of vampire fiction. I also find myself creating a number of characters in the novels that perhaps at first I don't realize are important, but later want to return to them in the series. That's what happened with the ghost hunters who now have their own novel and hopefully more. This gives me a lot of stories to play with.

Question: What makes your series unique?

Answer: Well, of the feedback I've gotten, it seems that along with fans of the genre, my novels have an appeal even to those who aren't that heavily (or aren't at all) into the genre. In fact, I've turned on a few people to the genre. I think that's due largely to the relationships in my novels and the humor within.

I also view the characters not necessarily as vampires struggling to regain their humanity, but as humans struggling with a very strange disease. Unlike diabetes, for example, vampirism is not a degenerative disease, quite the contrary. But like a disease such as diabetes, there are certain things that the vampire must be mindful of in his or her daily life for his survival as well as the survival of others he comes into contact with. There are realities to the condition that make it hard to navigate in normal society.

There's also the fact that the conversion is never a sure thing and a human might convert to a nearly mindless, wild vampire, or a sentient that is able to walk among normal without detection. Or anything in between (as the mutant Boris is). I think it adds for variety among the characters as well as future plots. I'm also mindful that a body does not change overnight. The vampires in my series "evolve" over the years, becoming stronger or more skilled with their abilities.

Question: Who is your favorite vampire?

Answer: It's very hard for me to pick a favorite anything because it all depends on my moods, but while he's not my favorite, I'm fascinated with Dracula because of the love affair the public has had with the character since the novel's publication. I mention this in *Vampires' Most Wanted*, but reading the novel, I found the character to be rather undefined in a lot of respects, but whether or not it was intentional (it might have been a result of the way the story was told), I think it was a brilliant move on Stoker's part. By making the character ambiguous, it opened it up for interpretations by later novel writers, screenwriters, etc., which helped keep the character fresh and alive (so to speak) as times changed. He can be anything the project calls for: a monster, a tortured soul, a romantic, even a bit comical, as George Hamilton proved. And this keeps him popular as times change.

If I had to choose, I think my favorite character would probably be Lestat. I think that's when I really fell in love with the genre. I enjoyed what Rice did with the idea of telling the story from the vampire's perspective, which was kind of revolutionary at the time. In the character of Lestat, you have the corruption of the need and the desire for redemption. Louis wars with it more, but as the later tales were told, we see a side of Lestat emerging that was never quite as at peace with his situation as he seemed to be.

If I had to pick a favorite scary vampire, I think it would be the vampires in *30 Days of Night* (curiously, I preferred the movie to the graphic novel, but I'm not a huge comic book/graphic novel fan). Predatory opportunists perhaps even more frightening in the fact that, wearing the clothes they do and almost passing for normal, you can actually see the humans they once were but are no longer.

Question: What are your favorite books to read?

Answer: I really liked the Anne Rice books. That would probably be my favorite series. I'm not a huge fan of romance books which often feature vampires. That's not to say I don't like romance in the books, but I prefer it subtly placed. I like a nice mix of drama, chills, romance, and humor. Some of the romance/erotic books seem simply to be excuses to get two people in bed. I want a plot. Some of the characters also seem a bit interchangeable.

One of my favorite books was *I Am Legend* by Richard Matheson. Very well done and an interesting take on the genre (again, another one of those "transition" pieces that helped take the vampire into new areas and keep it popular). And a series that really impressed me recently was The Strain series by

Guillermo del Toro and Chuck Hogan. It's very creepy and a nice little homage to *Dracula* in the beginning.

Question: If you use mythology in your books, what is it, why did you use it, and can you tell me in about a paragraph or two about this myth?

Answer: I cover some mythological aspects to vampirism in *Vampires' Most Wanted*. I decided to make the vampirism in The Khan Family Series a medical, not a supernatural, condition. I do have one of the vampires in the third novel mention being a child of Kali-ma. Kali (whom I mention in *Vampires' Most Wanted*) was the Hindu goddess of destruction and rebirth (a misunderstood goddess in the west). She was created to help the gods fight in a war against the demon Raktabija and his horde. Every time Raktabija was wounded, more demons sprang from drops of his blood, so Kali drained him of his blood and sucked up his demons. She then went on a rampage that was only stopped when her consort, Shiva, lay down among the bodies and, in her battle rage, she stepped on his chest. Realizing she had committed a terrible act of disrespect, her mind cleared. The concept of Kali is an interesting one, illustrating the destruction that often precedes creation. And it's very similar to the vampire in general; a character often created through an act of violence, large or small, that produces a whole new being.

Question: What are your favorite things about vampires in pop culture today?

Answer: I think the notion of the vampire as superhero. In my series, because they don't have to kill to survive (they do need human blood, which is where the inconvenience comes in) their condition doesn't alter their moral compass. They are who they were in that regard before the change. So you will have good people trying to do the best they can with a weird and sometimes dangerous condition. And you will have psychopaths who become even more dangerous because of the condition. In pop culture, it's kind of neat having a vampire use his skills for good to balance the scales after some of the more questionable stuff he's had to do to survive. It's also one of the evolutions of the creature that has helped it remain popular as times changed. I think there's room in the genre (and in a story) for a variety of vampires, whether they are decent people in untenable situations or full out monsters. And I think that's what makes the whole genre so interesting. There's a lot to choose from.

Question: What are your least favorite things about vampires in pop culture today?

Answer: Twilight. Enough said. Seriously, one of the things that bothers me about that series, and you see it in other young adult vampire stories, is the notion that a 100-plus-year-old vampire would be willing to hang out in high school. One reason I find Edward so very unappealing is the fact that even though he is a century old, he still often acts like a petulant teen. You mean to tell me there has been no growth of intellect or emotional maturity over the decades? Such a lifespan would have more of an impact on a personality than is perceptible in Twilight novels.

The other thing that sometimes annoys me is the absence of inconvenience. I like playing with inconveniences in my series because I feel that by presenting more things to challenge the characters, it offers more dramatic tension to the story. Lately, you see more and more inconveniences of being a vampire eroding to make the storytelling more convenient. In the TV show *Moonlight*, for example, the vampire could go out in the daylight as long as he wore sensible clothes. Now I know that the notion of a vampire burning in daylight really became popular with Nosferatu (though I think it existed in some legends prior to that). Dracula could go out in the daylight; he just lost some of his power during the day. But there you go: Dracula lost some of his power. He was weakened. More and more, you're seeing vampires who can hang out during the daylight and the most they have to worry about is applying some sunblock. The vamps in Twilight are beautiful people who live forever, who are very powerful, who are very wealthy, who can control their need for blood, and their biggest concern when it comes to sunlight is that they sparkle. It doesn't quite ooze dramatic tension.

Question: Where can we find you on the internet?

Answer: I'm on Facebook and Twitter @laura_enright or on my blog http://lauraenright.blogspot.com. Stop by and say "hi."

~Interview with Margarita Felices, author of *Judgement of Souls*~

Question: Tell me about yourself and why you wanted to write books about vampires.

Answer: I live in Cardiff, where my story is set, with my partner and three little mad dogs and I work for a well-known TV broadcasting company. I love living in Cardiff because, for all its modernization, there are still remnants of an old Victorian city. Cardiff has such character. When I can, I go out to the coast and take photographs; mind you, we have a lovely castle in the city centre and a fairytale one just on the outskirts, so when I feel I can't write anything, I take a ramble to those locations and it clears my head.

I suppose it was inevitable that someday I would write a novel. My teachers at school used to limit me to no more than ten pages. When I left school, I wrote short stories for magazines, and it paid my way through college. I am Gothic; I love the fashion, the architecture, and the music. The club in my novel is real. When I was writing Book One, I got all my club material and clientele from here. I wouldn't have finished that section without it.

There has always been a fascination in vampire stories and I wanted to write something different. I was fed up of the way women were portrayed as the weak female, so I decided to write about a strong, independent woman that was also a little vulnerable.

Question: What series do you write? Please describe it in one to two paragraphs.

Answer: I enjoy writing fiction and vampires are, and always will be, my favorite genre. When I started *Judgement of Souls*, I intended it to be a stand-alone book, but as the story progressed, it took on a life of its own and it needed to have a further story – a back story as to why it all happened and who started the whole upheaval in the vampire community, so it has now become a trilogy.

Question: Are your characters based off of any vampires in pop culture?

Answer: No, they are totally mine; they are the voices in my head, and the people I see in my dreams. Readers are aware of anything that resembles another character and will pull you on it. I didn't want that to happen, so I gave my characters different mannerisms that you wouldn't normally see in modern-day vampire stories.

Question: Are your books based off of any stories in pop culture?

Answer: No, I tried to stay original. My story is one that you will never have read before. It's hard to find a different angle when so much has been done already; it took time to get to know my characters before I wrote about them so I could get them just right and get their story just right and believable.

Question: What do you see in your future for your series?

Answer: My story is a trilogy. I intend to finish them all and then afterwards write about my two main characters from the first book (*JOS3/Rachel and Daniel*). They will be featured in a series of adventures with the two immortals helping to gather occult items from around the world. I work for television and, if I can, I intend to script one of the stories and submit it for perusal.

Question: What makes your series unique?

Answer: I've read so much vampire literature that I wanted a story to be totally different - this is not your ordinary vampire story. It's not all about blood-sucking beings. It's revenge, its romance, it's a treasure hunt for one of the most important vampire artifacts, and the winner will get the ultimate prize. I have written characters with a real history and also a common goal, mortal and immortal coming together, and you live with them in their journey. It has a different perspective from any vampire story that I have ever read.

Question: Who is your favorite vampire?

Answer: I am very partial to Lestat du Lioncourt (*Interview with the Vampire/Queen of the Damned/The Vampire Lestat*). He appears to be extremely arrogant, but in truth, he is frightened of being alone; saying that, he has a mistrust of everyone - mortal and immortal - so he is, in fact, his own worst enemy.

Question: What are your favorite books to read?

Answer: Anything supernatural–vampires, ghosts, witches, magic. I am a huge fan of Anne Rice and Stephen King. But I tend to read the back of a book and not care who's written it. The story is most important, one that can transport me to another existence is something that captivates me and as I have so little time these days, it has to be a special story.

Question: If you use mythology in your books, what is it, why did you use it, and can you tell me in about a paragraph or two about this myth?

Answer: I started with the story of Lilith because I find that the story of Lilith has been buried and religion does not recognize her even though she is written in several other religious bibles and in ancient Hebrew Scriptures. And the myths surrounding Cain were fascinating. I've read several papers with regards to Cain and his possible involvement in being the first vampire – so I just combined both stories. When I began to write the passages from the Book of Cain at the start of *JOS,* it made so much sense - but I take each story with a grain of salt.

Question: What are your favorite things about vampires in pop culture today?

Answer: Nothing is taboo any more. We have long portrayed the vampire as a blood-thirsty tyrant, but in modern-day stories, we can see them as elegant creatures; no longer are they hiding in dark corners, but they are out to play with mortals.

Question: What are your least favorite things about vampires in pop culture today?

Answer: Everyone wants to be a vampire! It is tiresome to read about people role-playing with fake fangs and having blood parties. It annoys me to read on different internet groups about blood lusting when it's not only about that. It ridicules the genre and makes them comical and it's no wonder that when a story comes to light, it is not taken seriously.

Question: Where can we find you on the internet?

Answer: I don't have a website yet – it is under construction. I have a Facebook and Amazon.com page.

~~Interview with Elizabeth Loraine, author of *The Royal Blood Chronicles*~~

Elizabeth Loraine, the author of The Royal Blood Chronicles Series, spoke with me about her series and how she came about writing vampire books.

The Royal Blood Series begins with the first book, *Katrina: The Beginning*. Katrina tells the story of a young royal vampire who finds out that she and her friends are destined to be the protectors of all the races in the world.

The second book, *The Protectors,* provides the backstory of each of the royal vampires' warriors. When speaking with Elizabeth, this is what she said about how she came about writing vampire books:

"I really decided on vampires because I love them, I always have. From Bela Lugosi to Bella Swan, but after reading most what's out there, I got bored. I wanted to know more than the modern high school vampire books were offering me.

What had these long-lived vampires been doing? What had they seen throughout history and how had it changed the way they saw the world around them. This was a niche I thought I could fill. Something different – a new vampire series, filled with a different vampire. Vampires as a race are not the usual undead, soulless beings. They've seen it all and found a way to not only survive, but thrive. Hiding in plain sight! And Royal Blood Chronicles was born. This series follows the Royal Blooded old world vampires trying to make the transition to the new world."

The series has been successful and she found what she wanted to create and has written more in the series. When asked where she got the idea for the series she said:

"The idea for Royal Blood Chronicles came out of what I was looking for as a vampire reader and couldn't find- strong female characters. No damsels in distress; tough, strong yet feminine characters. Beautiful women with a killer instinct and willing to fight for what they believed in. Women who chose men that complemented them, not dominated them."

The fans have absolutely loved the series. This is proven by the number of downloads that each of her books has had.

Elizabeth is very active on her Facebook and tries to answer all of her fans' questions and also takes their advice on things such as book covers and storylines.

She is one of the fastest rising young adult vampire authors, as evidenced by the popularity of the series. She published her first book in 2011 and has completed nine books in this series, a ghost and a shifter series as well as four novellas since then. She can be found at www.elizabethloraine.com

~Interview with Corvis Nocturnum, Occult Author and Publisher ~

Question: Corvis, can you tell me about yourself?

Answer: I am an author of many occult and subculture/pop cultural books for Schiffer Publishing and my own company, Dark Moon Press, started back in 2005. What some people don't know is I started out as an artist first and began writing later while recovering from an accident while working for Ingram Books. It seemed only natural that I write about the topics I do, simply based off my interests in the occult, vampires, zombies and horror in general. I still do artwork, much of it for hire for books, CDs, and commissioned work. I paint Gothic erotica and fantasy art in my spare time.

My educational background in the fields of Criminal Justice and Business Management has helped in business, of course, but I am using the legal aspects to see how I might assist various communities, such as alternative religions rights advocacy.

Question: How have you been able to share your knowledge with those that may not understand who you are and what you do?

Answer: Back in summer of 2006, I was an invited speaker at the 2006 World Religions Seminar at Indiana-Purdue University Fort Wayne, I have been a consultant in 2010 for A&E's *Paranormal States* episode "Satan's Soldier," and a guest panelist at Dragon Con 2011 in Atlanta, GA alongside paranormal and vampire authors such as Michelle Belanger and Rosemary Ellen Guiley.

This year, I was appointed as an official media representative for The Church of Satan, after I appeared on The BET Channel's episode of *The Lexi Show* on The Word Network. I was detailing the difference between Satanism as a religion versus Devil worship. I do my best to debunk the many myths and stereotypes prevalent about dark subcultures at conventions and universities.

I am also proud of having an appearances in magazines such as the October 2009 *Penthouse Magazine* article interview on sex and Satanism, *Philadelphia Weekly* as an artist at Germ Gallery and am an occasional writer for *Dark Resurrected Magazine*.

Question: Tell us more about Dark Moon Press and who you work with in the vampire and occult world.

Answer: Dark Moon Press has grown to over fifty titles in just seven years and nearly a dozen authors. We pride ourselves by being the best in occult, new age, horror, and paranormal books. Last year, we were picked up by Azure Green/Abyss Distribution as one of the largest middleman distribution centers in the world. I am proud to say we are always growing.

Question: What books have you written thus far?

Answer: My list of books are a bit lengthy and I am still working on some new ones, like a vampire myth and legends book for 2015, but this is the majority of them with dates:

- *Embracing the Darkness; Understanding Dark Subcultures*, (Dark Moon Press, 2005)
- *A Mirror Darkly*, (Dark Moon Press, 2006)
- *Promethean Flame*, (Dark Moon Press, 2008)
- *Allure of the Vampire; Our Sexual Attraction to the Undead*, (Dark Moon Press, 2009)
- *Cemetery Gates; Death and Mourning through the Ages*, (Schiffer Publishing, 2011)
- *I, Lucifer: Exploring the Archetype and Origins of the Devil*, (Schiffer Publishing, 2011)
- *Satan's Minions: Fallen Angels, Demons and Other Dark Creatures*, (Dark Moon Press, 2011)
- *Walking The Path Of The Ancient Ways: Pagans in Their Own Words*, Corvis Nocturnum and Andrieh Vitimus, (Dark Moon Press, 2012)
- Most Haunted: Scariest Places on Earth, Corvis Nocturnum (Dark Moon Press, 2012)
- Haunted Asylums, as E.R. Vernor (Schiffer Publishing, 2012)
- *Goth Girls, Vampire Vixens and Satan's Sirens*, Corvis Nocturnum and Old Nick Magazine, (Dark Moon Press, 2012)
- *Dark Visions: The Art of Corvis Nocturnum*, Corvis Nocturnum (Dark Moon Press, 2012)
- *Zombie Nation: from Folklore to Modern Frenzy*, E. R. Vernor (Schiffer Publishing, 2013)
- *Eerie America: Travel Guide of the Macabre*, E. R. Vernor and Kevin Eads, (Schiffer Publishing, 2013)

- *Vampire Evolution: Myth to Modern Day,* E. R. Vernor and Laura Carruba, (Schiffer Publishing, 2015)

Question: Where can we find out more about you and your books?

Answer: Our website is www.darkmoonpress.com and my website is www.corvisnocturnum.com . Please feel free to visit and ask me anything about what we have discussed above.

Question: Thank you for doing this and we look forward to reading more of your books.

~~~VAMPIRES IN FILM~~~

The Vampires in Film section provides the reader with lists of actors who played Dracula, a concise and personal favorite list from the more popular American cinema. There is also an essay focusing on the role of African-American vampires in film by BittenTwice. Enjoy this section and see just how many of these movies that you have viewed and how many will be moved to your "To Be Viewed" List."

~~Actors who have played Dracula in Movies and on Television~~

- Béla Lugosi-*Dracula* (1931), Abbott and Costello Meet Frankenstein (1948)
- Carlos Villarias- *Dracula* (1931) Italy
- Christopher Lee–*Horror of Dracula* (1958), *Dracula: Prince of Darkness* (1966), *Dracula Has Risen from the Grave* (1968), Count Dracula (1970), *Taste the Blood of Dracula* (1970), One More Time (1970), *Scars of Dracula* (1970), Dracula AD 1972* (1972), *Satanic Rites of Dracula* (1973), *Dracula and Son* (1976)
- Lon Chaney, JR–Son of Dracula (1943)
- Jon Carradine–*House of Frankenstein* (1944), **House of Dracula** (1945)
- Denholm Elliott - Mystery and Imagination (TV Series) (1966-1968)
- Jack Palance–*Bram Stoker's Dracula* (1973)
- Udo Kier – *Blood of Dracula* (1974)

-
- John Forbes Robertson - *The Legend of the 7 Golden Vampires* (1974)
- Louis Jourdan-*Count Dracula* (1977)
- Frank Langella- *Dracula* (1977)
- Michael Nouri – *Cliffhanger: the Curse of Dracula* 1979
- George Hamilton - *Love at First Bite* (1979)
- Duncan Regehr - *Monster Squad* (1987)
- Leslie Nielsen - *Dracula: Dead and Loving It* (1995)
- Gary Oldman - *Bram Stroker's Dracula* (1992)
- Gerard Butler - *Dracula 2000* (2000)
- Patrick Bergin - *Dracula* (2002) TV Movie
- Stephen Billington - *Dracula II: Ascension* (2003)
- Richard Roxburgh - *Van Helsing* (2004)
- Rutger Hauer - *Dracula III: Legacy* (2005)
- Dominic Purcell - *Blade: Trinity* (2004)
- Marc Warren – *Dracula* TV Series (2006)
- Keith- Lee Castle – *Young Dracula* (2006-2014)
- Jonathan Rhyes-Myers - *Dracula* NBC show (2012)

~~1900s Vampire Movies~~

- *A Polish Vampire in Burbank (1984)*
- *A Tale of a Vampire (1992)*
- *Abbott and Costello Meet Frankenstein (1948)*
- *Addicted to Murder (1995)*
- *Addicted to Murder: Tainted Blood (1998)*
- *American Vampire (1997)*
- *Andy Warhol's Blood for Dracula (1973)*
- *An American Vampire Story (1997)*
- *Because of Dawn (1988)*

- *Beverly Hills Vampire (1988)*
- *Blacula (1972)*
- *Blade (1998)*
- *Blood Moon (1971)*
- *Bordello of Blood (1996)*
- *Bram Stoker's Dracula (1974)*
- *Bram Stoker's Dracula (1992)*
- *Brides of Dracula (1960)*
- *Buffy the Vampire Slayer (1992)*
- *Castle of the Living Dead (1964)*
- *Children of the Night (1992)*
- *Club Vampire (1998)*
- *Count Dracula (1970)*
- *Count Dracula (1977)*
- *Count Yorga (1970)*
- *Countess Dracula (1970)*
- *Cronos (1993)*
- *Crypt of the Vampire (1960)*
- *Dance of the Damned (1988)*
- *Darkness (1992)*
- *Daughters of Darkness (1971)*
- *Daughters of Dracula (1973)*
- *Dawn (1990)*
- *Dead at Night (1996)*
- *Deadline (1980)*
- *Def by Temptation (1990)*
- *Demon Queen (1986)*
- *Dinner with the Vampire (1988)*
- *Doctor Vampire (1997)*
- *Dr. Dracula (1981)*
- *Dracula (1931)*
- *Dracula (1958)*
- *Dracula (1977)*

- *Dracula AD 1972 (1972)*
- *Dracula Has Risen from the Grave (1968)*
- *Dracula Rises from His Coffin (1982)*
- *Dracula Rising (1993)*
- *Dracula vs. Frankenstein (1970)*
- *Dracula, The Great Undead (1985)*
- *Dracula: Dead and Loving It (1995)*
- *Dracula: Prince of Darkness (1966)*
- *Dracula's Hair (1992)*
- *Dracula's Last Rites (1980)*
- *Dracula's Vampire Lust (1970)*
- *Dracula's Widow (1988)*
- *Dragon Against Vampire (1985)*
- *Embrace of the Vampire (1995)*
- *Fearless Vampire Killers (1966)*
- *Fright Night (1985)*
- *Fright Night 2 (1988)*
- *From Dusk til Dawn (1996)*
- *Ganja And Hess (1973)*
- *Ghost Fever (1987)*
- *Horror Of Dracula (1958)*
- *House of Dark Shadows (1970)*
- *House of Dracula (1945)*
- *I Married a Vampire (1987)*
- *Innocent Blood (1992)*
- *Interview with the Vampire (1994)*
- *John Carpenter's Vampires (1998)*
- *Kingdom of the Vampire (1991)*
- *Lifeforce (1985)*
- *Love at First Bite (1979)*
- *Love Bites (1988)*
- *Mama Dracula (1980)*
- *Mark of the Vampire (1935)*

- *Mr. Vampire (1986)*
- *My Best Friend is a Vampire (1988)*
- *My Grandpa is a Vampire (1992)*
- *Near Dark (1987)*
- *Night of Dark Shadows (1971)*
- *Nightlife (1989)*
- *Nosferatu (1922)*
- *Nosferatu: Phantom der Nacht (1979)*
- *Once Bitten (1985)*
- *Orgy of the Vampires (1965)*
- *Pale Blood (1991)*
- *Red Blooded American Girl (1999)*
- *Rockula (1989)*
- *Salem's Lot TV Movie (2004)*
- *Salem's Lot TV Movie(1979)*
- *Scars of Dracula (1970)*
- *Scream Blacula Scream (1973)*
- *Sleepwalkers (1992)*
- *Son of Dracula (1943)*
- *Son of Dracula (1974)*
- *Space Vampires/Life Force (1985)*
- *Subspecies (1991)*
- *Sundown: Vampire Retreat (1990)*
- *Tale of a Vampire (1992)*
- *Taste the Blood of Dracula (1970)*
- *Teenage Space Vampires (1998)*
- *Teen Vamp (1988)*
- *The Addiction (1995)*
- *The Demon Planet (1965)*
- *The Devil Vendetta (1986)*
- *The Fearless Vampire Killers (1967)*
- *The Hunger (1983)*
- *The Legend of the 7 Golden Vampires (1974)*

- *The Lost Boys (1987)*
- *The Monster Squad (1987)*
- *The Night Stalker (1971)*
- *The Night Strangler (1973)*
- *The Playgirls and the Vampire (1960)*
- *The Reflecting Skin (1991)*
- *Requiem for a Vampire (1971)*
- *The Return of Count Yorga (1971)*
- *The Return of the Vampire (1944)*
- *The Satanic Rites of Dracula (1973)*
- *The Seven Brothers meet Dracula (1974)*
- *The Seven Vampires (1985)*
- *The Shiver of the Vampires (1971)*
- *The Vampire Carmilla (1999)*
- *The Vampire Journals (1996)*
- *The Vampire Lovers (1970)*
- *Thirst (1979)*
- *To Die For (1989)*
- *To Sleep With a Vampire (1992)*
- *Transylvania 6-5000 (1985)*
- *Twins of Evil (1971)*
- *Vamp (1986)*
- *Vampire at Midnight (1988)*
- *Vampire Blues (1999)*
- *Vampire Circus (1972)*
- *Vampire Cop (1991)*
- *Vampire in Brooklyn (1995)*
- *Vampire Journals (1996)*
- *Vampire Vixens from Venus (1994)*
- *Vampire's Kiss (1989)*

~~2000s Vampire Movies~~

- *30 Days of Night (2007)*
- *Abraham Lincoln Vampire Hunter (2012)*
- *An Erotic Vampire in Paris (2002)*
- *Bitten (2008)*
- *Blade II (2002)*
- *Blade: Trinity (2004)*
- *Blood (2000)*
- *Blood Angels (2005)*
- *Blood for Irina (2012)*
- *Blood Rayne (2006)*
- *Blood: The Last Vampire (2009)*
- *Bram Stoker's Dracula's Curse (2006)*
- *Bram Stoker's Way of the Vampire (2005)*
- *Breaking Wind – Parody (2012)*
- *The Brotherhood II (2001)*
- *Byzantium (2013)*
- *Cirque du Freak: The Vampire's Assistant (2009)*
- *City of Bones (2014)*
- *Dance with a Vampyre (in production)*
- *Dark Prince: The True Story of Dracula (2000)*
- *Dark Shadows (2012)*
- *Darkness (2012)*
- *Daybreakers (2009)*
- *Destroy (in production)*
- *Dracula (in production)*
- *Dracula 2000 (2000)*
- *Dracula 3000 (2004)*
- *Dracula 3D (in production)*
- *Dracula II: Ascension (2003)*
- *Dracula III: Legacy (2005)*

- *Dracula Year Zero (in production)*
- *Dracula's Curse (2003)*
- *Dylan Doug: Dead of Night (2011)*
- *Embrace the Vampire (2013)*
- *Fright Night Remake (2011)*
- *Fright Night 2- Reimage (2013)*
- *Frost Bitten (2006)*
- *Hallow's End (2003)*
- *Harker (in production)*
- *High Midnight (2012)*
- *Hotel Transylvania (2012)*
- *House of Night (in production)*
- *I am Legend (2007)*
- *I Sell the Dead (2008)*
- *Immortal Kiss (2012)*
- *Innocence (2013)*
- *Jesus Christ Vampire Hunter (2001)*
- *John Carpenter's Los Muertos (2004)*
- *Kiss of the Damned (2013)*
- *Let Me In (2008)*
- *Let the Right One In (2010)*
- *Midnight Son (2011)*
- *Mom's Got a Date with a Vampire (2000)*
- *My Stepbrother is a Vampire (2013)*
- *Not Like Others (2008)*
- *Only Lovers Left Alive (2013)*
- *Phobia (2013)*
- *Priest (2011)*
- *Queen of the Damned (2002)*
- *Rise: Blood Hunter (2007)*
- *Shadow of the Vampire (2000)*
- *Stakeland (2011)*
- *Stan Helsing (2008)*

- *Stoker (2013)*
- *Terror of Dracula (2012)*
- *The Adventures of Young Helsing (2005)*
- *The Bloody Indulgent (2014)*
- *The Breed (2006)*
- *The Brides of Sodom (2013)*
- *The Brotherhood (2000)*
- *The Caretaker (2012)*
- *The Curse of Styria (2014)*
- *The Forsaken (2001)*
- *The Historian (2010)*
- *The Hunger 2 (2012)*
- *The Last Voyage of Demeter (in production)*
- *The Legend of Cain (in production)*
- *The Librarian: The Curse of the Judas Chalice (2008)*
- *The Lost Boys 2- The Tribe (2008)*
- *The Lost Boys 3- The Thirst (2010)*
- *The Monster Squad (in production)*
- *The Night Stalker (in production)*
- *The Passage (2013)*
- *The Redemption of Cain (in production)*
- *The Thompsons (2012)*
- *Thirst (2009)*
- *True Blood Thirst SyFy Movie (2012)*
- *Twilight (2008)*
- *Twilight: Breaking Dawn 2 (2012)*
- *Twilight: Breaking Dawn 1 (2011)*
- *Twilight: Eclipse (2010)*
- *Twilight: New Moon (2009)*
- *Ultraviolet (2006)*
- *Underworld (2003)*
- *Underworld : Evolution (2006)*
- *Underworld: Awakening (2012)*

- *Underworld: Rise of the Lycans (2009)*
- *Vamp U (2013)*
- *Vampire Academy (2014)*
- *Vampire Boys (2010)*
- *Vampire Boys 2 (2012)*
- *Vampire Clan (2002)*
- *Vampire Dog (2012)*
- *Vampire Hunter D (2001)*
- *Vampires (2010)*
- *Vampires : Out for Blood (2004)*
- *Vampires Anonymous (2003)*
- *Vampires Los Muertos (2002)*
- *Vampires Suck (2010)*
- *Vampires vs. Zombies (2011)*
- *Vampires: The Turning (2005)*
- *Vamps (2013)*
- *Van Helsing (2004)*
- *Van Helsing (in production)*
- *Vlad (2003)*
- *Way of the Vampire (2005)*

~~List of Vampire Movies and Television Shows featuring Black Actors~~

- *Blacula* 1972. William Marshall plays Prince Mamuwalde, the ruler of an African nation, who seeks the help of Count Dracula to help stop the slave trade. Dracula, who, along with his other evils, is revealed as a racist, not only refuses to help, but also transforms Mamuwalde into a vampire and renames him Blacula. It is the first of the blaxpoitation horror films.

- *Ganja and Hess* 1973. Archaeologist Dr. Hess Green becomes a vampire after being stabbed with an ancient cursed dagger by his assistant. He then falls in love with his assistant's widow, Ganja. The film stars Marlene Jones and Duane Gunn.
- *Vamp* 1986. Stars Grace Jones as a vampire who challenges fraternity boys to survive until dawn.
- *Def by Temptations* 1990. Kadeem Hardison and Samuel L. Jackson play in this low budget failed movie where a succubus is attacking young black men. The succubus is played by Cynthia Bond.
- *Vampire in Brooklyn* 1995. Sexy Eddie Murphy plays Maximillian, a vampire who is searching for his soul mate, NYPD officer Rita Veder.
- *Kindred: the Embraced* 1996. Erik King plays the Detective Sonny Toussaint, a vampire who helps protect the masquerade of the vampires. This television show ended after the first season after the real life death of the lead actor, Mark Frankel.
- The Blade Trilogy: *Blade* 1998, *Blade II* 2002, and *Blade Trinity* 2004. Wesley Snipes plays Blade, a daywalker. This sexy vampire has some of the qualities of vampires, such as the need for blood, with being able to walk in the sunlight. *Blade* was probably the first movie to really draw attention to the black vampire as a sex symbol as well as serious vampire movie.
- *Dracula 2000* 2000. Marcus, played by Omar Epps, is a supporting character in this story of how Dracula came to be.
- *Queen of the Damned* 2002. Aaliyah, singer and actress, portrayed Queen Akasha, the Mother of all Vampires. Lestast's music wakens the Queen and the story begins. This film is based on Anne Rice's

Vampire Chronicle Series. This was the actress's last movie because she was killed during filming.

- *Underworld* 2003. Robbie Gee played Kahn, the weapons master for the Death Dealers.
- *Twilight* 2008 and *New Moon* 2009. Edi Gathergi who plays Laurent, a member of the "bad" vampires in Twilight, was a wonderful sight on screen. His six-pack abs, long hair, and stunning eyes make him very sexy.
- *Twilight: Breaking Dawn Part 2* 2012. This movie introduced beautiful black women into modern vampire movies. The members of the Amazon tribe that comes to aid the Cullens are Zafrini played by Judith Shekoni, a British actress, and Senna played by Tracey Heggins.
- *The Originals* 2014-present Marcel played by Charles Michael Davis. He is sired by Klaus and in the beginning was the King of New Orleans. He is also the past lover of Rebekkah.

~~Reviews of Vampire Movies~~

~Vampire Movies of 2011 brought a variety of types to the big screen~

Vampire fans had just a handful of vampire films to go see at the theaters in 2011. *Twilight: Breaking Dawn Part 1, Priest, Fright Night,* and *Dylan Dog.* These were a perfect range of romance, comedy, traditional horror, and even a cult classic remake. 2011 brought a vampire movie for each type of vampire lover out there. Here they are, as they appeared at the theaters.

Dylan Dog: Dead of Night was released in April 2011. It had just the perfect mix of comedy, horror, and mystery. Dylan is a private investigator that used to look into things that "have no pulse." His best friend and business partner becomes a zombie and he meets the most unusual vampires and werewolves. It is reminiscent of the 80s vampire comedies like *My Best Friend is a Vampire* and *Once Bitten.* It showed how much fun a vampire movie could be without being too stiff or too slapstick.

In May, the vampire movie went darker and more monstrous than the previous one. *Priest* is definitely the most traditional vampire release of the year. It is what many of the vampire fans have been missing at the theaters. It is a great story with a lot of action. It tells the story of a priest who goes against the church when his niece is kidnapped. The old setting and the romance, blood, and story are wonderful. It was a good representation of the more horror-related movies.

August brought about a movie with the most mix of reviews, the remake of the 80s cult film *Fright Night.* Loyal *Fright Night* fans were adamant about their hatred for this film. Originally, there had been hope that this would bring in the fans of the original movie and also introduce it to a new generation, but unfortunately, this did not happen. It actually was not seen by several original fans and the new ones the production company was seeking didn't show up at the box office. *Fright Night* brought Colin Ferrell into his first vampire role as Jerry Dandridge, the creepy neighbor who is killing young females in the town. Anton Yelchin plays Charley Brewer, the nerdy teen who realizes what is happening. He and his friends must try and save the town from the sexy, blood-sucking demon.

But come November, the box office exploded with Twi-hards, Twi-moms, and poor boyfriends who were dragged to the theater to see Edward's and Bella's wedding, honeymoon, and birth of their child. *Twilight: Breaking Dawn Part 1,* brought in over $650,000,000 worldwide and was the number one movie for four weeks in a row. Its success is attributed to the mass following of not just the books or movies, but also of the actors. *Breaking Dawn, Part 1* is the first installment of the final vampire book in Stephenie Meyer's Twilight series. It tells the story of the wedding and honeymoon of vampire Edward and human Bella, and ends with the horrific pregnancy and impending doom of the cast that was shown in the conclusion of the this movie series. Many fans were upset over the ending of the movie because it put a unique spin on the book ending. Reviewers have said that the movies have become increasingly better since the first Twilight release. It is a Romeo and Juliet story that causes people to argue the positive and negative messages in the film, and whether Bella is a good role model for young teens.

2012 brought forth box office winners *Hotel Transylvania, Dark Shadows, Underworld: Awakening, Abraham Lincoln: Vampire Hunter* and of course *Twilight: Breaking Dawn part 2* being released and once again taking the theaters by storm. See below some of the reviews courtesy of the Vampire Examiner on Examiner.com.

~*Abraham Lincoln: Vampire Hunter*~

Abraham Lincoln: Vampire Hunter succeeds in connecting history with mythology. It was a unique and fresh story of both history and mythology.

The author of the book, Seth Grahame-Smith, was also the screenwriter of the movie. And he succeeded in researching and keeping as close to history as possible.

The death of Abe's mother was one note in history that Smith wrote into the movie that worked wonderfully. In reality, Nancy died of milk consumption, a disease that caused the body to become really pale and resemble a vampire. In the movie, Nancy was killed by a vampire. The two symptoms were so similar that the rewriting of history was simple here.

Another example of the rewriting of history for the movie was the Civil War and the connection of vampires to slavery. The movie used the idea that the plantation owners and the government would bring slaves to the south for food for vampires to satiate them and to keep them in one area. This was a very intriguing and unique idea. It really paralleled the atrocities and horrors of slavery and the idea that not just African-Americans, but all men were to be slaves to these monsters.

Other than the interest of historical facts and events, the resurrection of traditional vampires has returned to the movie screen. Smith delivered a story of vampires that really connected with traditional vampires. They were brutal, blood thirsty, power hungry, and powerful – what a true vampire is.

But, of course, he did add the vampire who hated who he was and wanted redemption. Henry was a mixture of a character that you hated, felt sorry for, and distrusted from the beginning. It seems that most movies must have this redeeming vampire character that has to sacrifice who they want to be for some idea of good, and then balance himself between the world of good and evil.

The characters were portrayed wonderfully. Mary Todd was portrayed as a strong female who could not only read Lincoln, but also be strong and passionate. She was just the opposite of so many of the female characters that are written as whiny and weak.

Lincoln was portrayed very much like I thought he would be. He was very straight forward and focused on his job either as a hunter or a president. They did show his connection to family and love, but did not portray him as too much one way or the other. He is who he is, and that is it. This is what made this portrayal a success.

Abraham Lincoln: Vampire Hunter was full of emotions, passion, action, and blood. It is a must see for any vampire lover. It is a movie that will not disappoint those that have been waiting for a traditional vampire story to return to the movie screen.

~*Dark Shadows* is a Fresh Take on a Cult Classic~

Tim Burton's *Dark Shadows* was a refreshing look at the 1960s cult classic. Burton did well with showing the history of Barnabas Collins and the curse from the witch Angelique.

He introduced the first meeting of Barnabas and Angelique as a simple glimpse and interest of two children in different social circles. The look between the two characters easily shows the passion that the two would have as adults.

The human life of Barnabas was interesting. It showed Barnabas as a ladies' man who threw away women's hearts like the daily trash. It was a very good background story to Barnabas' curse and showed that he had a lot to learn.

Barnabas as a vampire was great. He actually drank blood and killed people, a refreshing idea for vampire movies today. He had blood on his face, he compelled people, and he sought vengeance when he needed it. He was a monster, but also a monster that did love, as true to the story of *Dracula*.

The movie was funny as well. Barnabas' encounters with the future people and gadgets were some of the funniest scenes in the movie. But, my most favorite was his time around the campfire with the hippies. It started out as funny and even deeply emotional. but ended violently, a perfect mix, just like the television show.

The soundtrack was great. The sex scenes were perfect. The interaction between the Collinses and Barnabas was wonderful. We all know that Burton tells a good story, but doesn't go into depth, so no one should be surprised that the character weren't extremely deep.

But, my favorite character was Caroline. I do hope that in the sequel that they will show more of her. According to the last screen shot, the psychiatrist may be Barnabas' next love-stricken vixen.

If you love action, romance, and comedy all rolled into one, then this is the perfect fun vampire movie for you.

~Interview with Actor and Vampire Santa, Sal Lizard~

In 2010, I was attending ScareFest, a horror and paranormal convention in Lexington, KY, when I passed the table of this gentleman who looked like Santa Claus. I was intrigued. He smiled at me and I was in awe when I saw fangs glistening. I immediately ran up to him and introduced myself. He was an interesting man; a little uhm… frisky… and, well, fun! Earlier this year, I ran into him again at Dead Winter Con in London, KY, and he agreed to do an interview for me.

Be prepared, though! He is not your ordinary Santa, nor is he your ordinary vampire. Be prepared; I have warned you.

Question: Sal, can you please tell us about yourself.

Answer: My name is Sal Lizard and I am an actor. I have played parts in several horror films, but I am known best for my Santa roles.

I am a professional real beard Santa. I play Santa at the malls, in parades, in nursing homes, and even visit kids in their homes. I have even been in a few movies such as *The Box* and *I Don't Know How She Does It*.

I was also elected as the Commander of Starfleet, the International Star Fleet Fan Association from 2007-2010.

But, my most recent role in movies and at conventions has been as "Vampire Santa."

Question: Where are you from? I see the Santa Mobile all around Kentucky, Ohio, and Tennessee.

Answer: Where is MY North Pole? Isn't that a little personal *wink*. I call North Hampton my current home and also have a home on Brunswick, GA. But, I am never in "anyplace" for more than a couple of months a year. I am almost always on the road, auditioning for parts, doing conventions, producing films, and finding investors. I have been averaging about 4,000 miles a month on my car, but gas prices have been slowing me down.

Question: How did you come up with the idea of "Vampire Santa"?

Answer: People always ask "What is Santa doing at a horror convention?" Once, when I brought the suit to a horror convention, everybody wanted their picture taken with me. I wanted to make Santa "fit in." I had the teeth already and I had the lenses, so I put them all together and the Vampire Santa was born. By making him a vampire, he has a place there too. Besides, vampires are seductive, sexual beings: it allows me to flirt with gals and be a little more "adult" with my humor.

Question: What is the strangest or wildest thing that you have been asked to do as Vampire Santa?

Answer: I've been asked to bite or lick some interesting places for photos, I've "motor-boated" a few gals, and I've been asked to attend a few "adult-oriented" parties! Did I tell you how much I love being the Vampire Santa?

Question: Do you have any upcoming events?

Answer: With increased popularity comes increased opportunity. I am getting into more and more horror conventions and events. I am also raising money for several film projects (investors: call me!) and there are two screenplays being developed around my Vampire Santa character. My new book comes out in November and I will be appearing on nationally-televised programs and at book-signings to promote it.

Question: What kind of events do you like to do? Can we request you some way?

Answer: I am available for booking at any horror or paranormal convention, movies, and more. I am available for private adult parties too.

Question: I have seen you, Sal, and you are a sexy vampire Santa and we all know that vampires are sexy. So, you are up for a few personal adult entertainings too? Well, how do we get in touch with you for any of these events?

Answer: My website is www.sallizard.com and my appearances are on www.actorsal.com. You can email me at sal@sallizard.com or call me at 740-601-7263.

~~~VAMPIRES ON TELEVISION~~~

The vampire may be eternal in books and on film, but when it comes to television, they often suffer a short life. Whether it was CBS's *Moonlight*, Lifetime's *Blood Ties*, ABC's *The Gates*, and Fox's *Kindred the Embraced*, the vampire TV show has anything but an eternal life.

In the late 1990s and early 2000s, our lovely creature of the night did enjoy a very long-lived life that turned into syndication in regards to *Buffy the Vampire Slayer* and *Angel*. However, while it was a wonderful gift from Joss Whedon, that was not the norm. in the 2000s, HBO's *True Blood*, CW's *The Vampire Diaries*, and both BBC's and SyFy's *Being Human* tried to break the records that *Buffy* and *Angel* have set.

After looking at record views, it appears that *True Blood* and *The Vampire Diaries* have broken this bad luck streak. Until *Game of Thrones, True Blood* was the most watched show on HBO and is a hit for adult viewers only. They have won both Emmy and Golden Globe awards. But, it was announced that its last season will be its seventh season, which will end in August of 2014.

The Vampire Diaries is the *True Blood* for those of a younger viewing audience, ranging from teens to thirty-year-olds. The show has been renewed for a fifth season that will premiere this fall. The show has garnered over three million viewers and has won People's Choice Awards and Teen Choice Awards. It garnered a spin off series titled, *The Originals,* which is geared towards the adult audience by leaving behind the high school setting and settling in hot New Orleans. *The Originals* has also been renewed for a second season.

But, even with the success that television shows have seen since the mid 1990s, it appears that this spell that vampires have had on television viewers is dwindling. In just the last two years, BBC's *Being Human*, Syfy's *Being Human*, NBC's *Dracula,* and HBO's *True Blood* have been cancelled. The two The CW shows are all that remain, except for the FX's shot at a new show called *Strain* that is seeing poor results. So, as mentioned in the introduction, it does appear that there is a huge decrease in movies, books, and television shows relating to vampires. So, let's see how long it takes for them to revert back into the coffin on the television scene. It looks like it is coming soon.

~~Vampire Television Shows~~

- *Angel (1999-2004)*
- *Being Human SyFy (2011- 2014)*
- *Being Human British (2008-2013)*
- *Blade the Series (2006)*
- *Blood+ (2005)*
- *Blood Ties (2006-2007)*
- *Buffy the Vampire Slayer (1997-2003)*
- *Cliffhanger: the Curse of Dracula (1979)*
- *Dark Shadows (1966-1971)*
- *Dark Shadows Remake (1991)*
- *Dracula NBC (2013- 2014)*
- *Dracula(1973) television movie*
- *Dracula a television adaptation of Bram Stoker's novel*
- *Dracula, part of the series Mystery and Imagination(1968)*
- *Dracula the Series (1990)*

- *Forever Knight (1989 movie 1992-1996)*
- *From Dusk til Dawn (2014-present)*
- *Helsing (2001)*
- *Kindred the Embraced (1996)*
- *Kolchak The Night Stalker (1974-1975)*
- *Moonlight (2007-2008)*
- *Mockingbird Lane (2012-pilot only)*
- *Preacher (possible but not picked up yet)*
- *Sanctuary (2008-2011)*
- *The Addams Family (1964-1966)*
- *The Gates (2010)*
- *The Munsters (1964-1966)*
- *The Originals (2013-present)*
- *True Blood (2008-2014)*
- *Ultraviolet (1998)*
- *Vampire Diaries (2009-present)*
- *Vampire High (2001-2002)*
- *Vampire Knight (2008)*
- *Young Dracula (2006-2014)*

~~Television Shows where a vampire appears in a single episode~~

- *Aqua Team Hunger Force*
- *Charmed*
- *Community*
- *Demons*
- *Doctor Who*
- *Futurama*
- *Gilligan's Island*
- *Murder She Wrote*
- *Robot Chicken*

- *Scrubs*
- *Superboy*
- *Supernatural*
- *The Dresden Files*
- *The Family Guy*
- *The Murdoch Mysteries*
- *The Simpsons*

~~Did You Know~~

- On April 14, 2012, Jonathan Frid, who played the sexy Barnabas Collins on *Dark Shadows*, died at the age of eighty-seven of natural causes in an Ontario, Canada hospital. He had been making appearances at the Dark Shadow Festival up until last year. Many *Dark Shadows* fans have followed him from the *Dark Shadows* days and view him as one of the best vampires of all time.

~~~VAMPIRES FOR CHILDREN~~~

Imagine going into a store and asking for vampire items for kids. Whether it is a preschool or easy reader book or a cartoon DVD, adults will give you a strange look when you have an armful of vampire items for children.

The comment that comes up the most is: "I didn't know that there were vampires for kids. Isn't it too scary and violent? I would never let my child have stuff that has vampires in it."

I just laugh at this because most of the vampire related items for children are items that most parents don't even realize that their own children are watching.

The question that I place to these parents is, "Has your child ever watched *Sesame Street* or *Scooby Doo?*" Well, then, your child has been exposed to the creepy monster known as the vampire.

I recently bought a book titled *Dick and Jane and Vampires* for my nephew for Christmas. I opened the book to the very picture that showed the kids running away from the vampire, screaming. Wow – that wouldn't win anyone over. As I flipped through the book, I noticed most of the pictures looked like that, until you read the accompanying text. The children were learning that not everything they see is as it appears. But to a parent just opening the book, it was not proving my point at all. It actually looked scary.

And what was my point? My point was that not all things are what they appear to be. There is a vampire for children that is age appropriate and facilitates learning. However, many adults just think about sharing their interest with their children with age-appropriate material. Being a former public school teacher, I stress, appropriate age-related material here.

In this section, you the reader will find a small list of child appropriate shows and books for children as well as an essay discussing how children have befriended the vampire.

~~Children's Cartoons, Television Shows and Movies~~

- *Attack of the Killer Tomato*
- *Count Duckula*
- *Dingbat and the Creeps*
- *Drak Pack*
- *Gravedale High*
- *Hotel Transylvania*
- *Little Dracula*
- *Mad Monster Party*
- *Mina and the Count*
- *Mona the Vampire*
- *Monster High*
- *Monster Squad*
- *Monster Tails*
- *My Babysitter's a Vampire*
- *Quacula*
- *Scary Godmother*
- *Scooby Doo and the Ghoul School*
- *Scooby Doo and the Legend of the Vampire*
- *Scooby Doo and the Legend of Vampire Rock*

- *Scooby Doo and the Reluctant Werewolf*
- *Sesame Street*
- *The Addams Family*
- *The Addams Family Cartoon*
- *The Batman vs Dracula: The Animated Movie*
- *The Groovie Ghoulies*
- *The Little Vampire*
- *The Munsters*
- *Vanpires*
- *Vampires, Pirates, and Aliens*
- *Young Dracula*

~~Cartoons that feature a vampire in some episodes~~

- *Animaniacs*
- *Captain N: The Game Master*
- *Codename Kids Next Door*
- *Digimon*
- *Duck Tales*
- *Greg the Bunny*
- *Looney Tunes*
- *Pokemon*
- *Super Friends*
- *The Comic Strip*
- *The Electric Company*
- *The Grimm Adventures of Billy and Mandy*
- *The Super Mario Brothers Super Show*

~~Children's Books for ages 6-12~~

- *A Night in the Lonesome October* by Roger Zelazny
- *A Practical Guide to Vampires* by Lisa Trumbauer
- *A Vampire Halloween* by John Bianchi

- *A Vampire is Coming to Dinner* by Pamela Jane and Pedro Rodriquez
- *A Vampire Named Fred* by Bill Crider
- *Alex Van Helsing* by Jason Henderson
- *Anno Dracula* by Kim Newman
- *Attack of the Vampire Weenie* by Brian Lubar
- *Baby Vampire Gulp!* by Lucie Papaneau et al
- Bunnicula Series by James Howe
- *Camp Vampire* by Jeff Gilbert
- *Captain Britain And MI13, Vol. 3: Vampire State* by Paul Cornell
- *Children of the Dragon: Illustrated Vampire Quartet* by Antellus
- *Children's Vampire Hunting Brigade*
- *Deathly Pale* by Anthony Paolucci
- *Dick, Jane and Vampires* by Laura Marchesni
- *Dracula* by Keith Faulkner and Jonathan Lambert
- *Essential Tomb of Dracula, Vol. 1* by Marv Wolfman
- *Fang of the Vampire* by Tommy Donvaband
- *Help! A Vampire is Coming* by Abby Klein
- *Horrid Henry and the Vampire Zombie* by Francesca Simon
- *How to be a Vampire* by R.L. Stein
- *Iris Investigates: Beastly Goings On In Pelican Wharf* by David Jacks
- *Josie Griffin is Not a Vampire* by Heather Swain
- *Little Vampire* by Joann Sfar
- *My Boyfriend is a Vampire* by Yu-Rang Han
- *My Dentist Is a Vampire* by M. T. Coffin
- *My Sister the Vampire* by Sienna Mercer
- *Nancy Drew, Vampire Slayer* by Stefan Petrucha
- *Night's Children: The Vampire* by Wendy Snow Lang
- *Notes from a Totally Lame Vampire* by Andrew Pniter

- *Prince of Dorkness* by Tim Collins
- *Priscilla the Great Vampire* by Sybil Nelson
- *Return of the Vampire* by Geronimo Stilton
- Scream Street Series by Tommy Donvaband
- *Sleepover Club Vampire* by Fionna Cummins
- *Space Camp Vampire* by Edward Packard
- *Teddy Gyros: Kid Vampire Slayer* by Michael Sortino
- *The Dancing Vampire* by Roberto Pavanello
- *The History of Vampires* by Sylvia Branzei
- The Little Vampire Series by Angela Sommer-Bodenburg
- *The Little Vampires* by Rebecca Hicks
- The Shadow Garden Series by Malla Duncan
- *The Sleepless Little Vampire* by Richard Egielski
- *The Story of Frankenstein Dracula and Wolfman* – no author listed
- *The Thief of Always* by Clive Barker
- *The Vampire Mystery: The Boxcar Children* by Gertrude Chandler Warner
- *The Vampire's Curse* by Dan Greenburg
- *The Vampire's Vacation* by Ron Roy
- *The Vampires Christmas* by Joseph Michael Linsner
- *The Vampires Went Thataway* by Nancy Lamb
- *The Vanishing Vampire: A Monsterrific Tale* by David Lubar
- *The Young Vampire Adventures* by Star Donovan
- *V is for Vampire* by Adele Griffin
- *Vampirates* by Justin Somper
- *Vampire Bass* by Tom Watson
- *Vampire Boy's Goodnight* by Lisa Brown
- *Vampire Brat* by Angie Sage
- *Vampire Breathe* by R.L. Stine
- *Vampire Don't Wear Polka Dots* by Debbie Dadey

- *Vampire Hunt* by Dan Jolley
- *Vampire Island* by Adele Griffin
- *Vampire Rising* by Jason Henderson
- *Vampire Snacks* by Larry Derryberry
- *Vampires* by Charlotte Guillain
- *Vampires* by Jim Pipe
- *Vampires* by S.L. Hamilton
- *Vampires!* by Steven Roberts
- *Vampires* by Stephen Krensky
- *Vampires Do Hunt Marshmallow Bunnies* by Marcia Thorton Jones
- *Vlad the Drac, Vampire* by Ann Jungman
- *Vinny the Vampire* by Jordan Pierce

~The Monster Becomes a Friend: The Vampire's Influence on Children~

The last two decades have brought about a welcoming of vampires in society. Long gone are the days of children cowering in the dark from fear of the vampire. The 1970s opened the door to change that not only affected the image of the vampire, but how we accepted them into our lives. From enticing young children to learning new academic and social skills and assisting teens to solve everyday issues and exploring who they are, the vampire has been the constant through each stage of social development.

In the past, vampires were portrayed as the rat, like Nosferatu or the strange, foreign-speaking Bela Lugosi-style vampire. However, today, they are portrayed as the cute Count von Count on *Sesame Street* or the sexy Edward of the teen series *Twilight*. This familiarization with the vampire has resulted in the instant recognition and acceptance of the once monstrous creature. They have been accepted into our daily society and no longer have to be explained or labeled; we simply know by sight that the creature on the television or in the description of a character in a book is a vampire. An example of this is a Ray Ban commercial that can be found on YouTube.

The scene: A couple of pairs of young twenty-somethings are sitting on the steps outside, just before the sun begins to rise. They look at each other and put on their Ray Ban sunglasses. One guy walks up to the group of friends and sits with them. He begins to look for his glasses, but can't find them. The sun rises and strikes the newcomer, who then turns into a pile of dust. One of the female characters says, "Looks like someone forgot his Ray Bans." The group laughs and they flash their vampire fangs.

The commercial assumes that the audience knows, through socialization of the vampire into culture, that this group of twenty-year-olds is vampires because they have fangs. They also expect us to see the humor in the unprepared guy turning to dust because we know that a vampire will turn to dust in the sunlight. Simply put, everyone knows what a vampire is through simple phrases or placement of symbols. Children and teens are not immune to this knowledge through various forms of pop culture and are readily accepting of this icon that has inundated their world.

In 1971, General Mills introduced a new cereal that was marketed with the idea to "bring monsters into your breakfast every day." The first of six monster-themed cereals were Count Chocula, a Nosferatu-looking vampire that was painted as rather comical looking. The Count would yell, "I vant to eat your cereal." As a result, the adults fled in fear, but the children invited him and his friends, Franken Berry, Boo Berry, and Yummy Mummy in to enjoy breakfast, the most important meal of the day. The vampire was no longer scary to children and would become the first part of every child's day, or so hoped General Mills. Count Chocula cereal is still available today in limited areas, but makes a special appearance at Halloween along with his other monster friends.

After children were finished eating their cereal, the next step in their morning would be to turn on the television to an educational program such as Sesame Street. Here, children would learn their colors, alphabet, and shapes. In 1972, a new character was introduced that would help children learn to count, a Bela Lugosi-looking vampire named Count von Count. He was obsessed with counting and would count anything that came his way. He would even count himself if there was nothing to count. Children would laugh at his spooky castle and coffin while learning these skills. The writers of the show based their character's obsession with counting on the myth of how to escape a vampire. The folktale says that in order to escape a vampire, one must drop seeds as they run because the vampire is obsessed with counting and would have to stop and count before continuing the chase. This was how the Count came to be. He was silly and obsessive, yet smart. He lived in a castle with his pet bats and was friends with the other characters on *Sesame Street.* Children learned their numbers while imitating his loud crackly laugh that resulted in lightning strikes and thunder claps. The Count was not scary, but a very good educational resource that children still enjoy today.

As children grew older, they began to read and, in 1979, *Bunnicula* was introduced to them. *Bunnicula*, a beginning reader book, was written by husband and wife team, Deborah and James Howe, and told the story of a cute bunny that is also a vampire. Bunnicula is adopted into a new home where the other pets, a cat and dog, are fearful and not accepting of him. Through different adventures, the cat and dog finally accept the "different" and "new" member of the family. This was a perfect story for teaching children to learn to accept differences in other children as well as address the rising issue of divorce and mixed families in the late 70s and early 80s. The cute bunny was successful in its popularity with children and is still in print with new releases today.

Children continue to learn diversity and friendship skills. The popularity of the television as a babysitter allowed the vampire to enter the home more often and, as a result, become a cute friend. The institutions of family and education rely on the media to socialize children and as a result of supply and demand, children turn to the vampire as a means of learning and growing. The vampire is now a friend and no longer a monster to be feared.

~~~VAMPIRES IN RECREATION~~~

The love for vampires has transcended from the page and screen into each fan's life. Fans love the creature of the night so much that many have found ways to make them seem more "real" to them and accessible in their daily lives.

Many fans have decided to join clubs so that they may meet others who have shared their interest in vampires. For example, the Camarilla Fan Club was founded because there were not only national but international fans of the *Vampire: The Masquerade Role Playing Game*. White Wolf, the creator of the game, now oversees this club that has thousands of members in countries all across the world.

This section provides links to fan clubs, card, video, and role-playing game websites as well as a very entertaining and informative interview with Hugo Pecos, the creator of The Federal Vampire and Zombie Agency.

~~Fan Clubs~~

- Anne Rice Vampire Lestat Fan Club
  www.vampirelestatfanclub.com
- The Dark Shadows Fan Club
  www.darkshadowsfestival.com

~~Role Playing and Table Top Games~~

- *Chill: Adventures into the Unknown* www.waynesbooks.com
- *Crimson Moon* www.cmrpg.net/
- *Nightlife* http://tritacgames.com/nightlife.htm
- *Reign of Blood* www.reignofblood.net
- *Vampire Kingdom-* www.palladiumbooks.com
- *White Wolf- Vampire Requiem* www.white-wolf.com
- *White Wolf Vampire The Masquerade* www.white-wolf.com

~~Video Games~~

- *A Vampyre Story* 2008
- *Blade* 2000
- *Bloodnet* 1993
- *BloodRayne* series 2002, 2004
- *Bram Stoker's Dracula* 1993
- *Buffy* series 2000–2009
- *Castlevania* series 1986–present
- *Countdown Vampires* 1999
- *Dark Angel: Vampire Apocalypse* 2001
- *Dark Legends* 2012
- *Darkwatch* 2005
- *Dracula* 1986
- *Dracula 2*: The Last Sanctuary 2000
- *Dracula 3*: The Path of the Dragon 2008
- *Dracula Unleashed* 1998
- *Dracula: Origin* 2008
- *Dracula: Resurrection* 1999

- *Elvira Mistress of the Dark* 1990
- *Fallout 3* 2008
- *Fortune Arterial* 2008
- *From Dusk Till Dawn* 2001
- *Ghost House* 1986
- *Gothos* 1997
- *Infamous 2: Festival of Blood* 2011
- *Last Flight* Unreleased
- *Legacy of Kain* series 1996–2003
- *Master of Darkness* 1992
- *Necrovision* 2009
- *Night of the Raving Dead* 2008
- *Nightrap* 1992
- *Nosferatu: The Wrath of Malachi* 2003
- *Skyrim* 2011
- *The Adventures of Shuggy* 2011
- *The Astonishing Adventures of Mr. Weems and the She Vampires* 1987
- *The Count* 1981
- *The Elder Scrolls IV: Oblivion* 2011
- *The Twisted Tales of Spike McFang* 1993
- *Vampire Hunter D* 1999
- *Vampire Night* 2000
- *Vampire Rain* 2007
- *Vampire Rush* 2011
- *Vampire Season* 2012
- *Vampire the Masquerade Bloodlines* 2004
- *Vampire the Masquerade Redemption* 2000
- *Vampire Village* 1983
- *Van Helsing* 2004
- *Veil of Darkness* 1993

~~Review of *The Tarot of the Vampyre* by Ian Daniels~~

The Tarot of the Vampyre by Ian Daniels is a beautiful but intense tarot deck that shows both the light and the shadow aspects of the questioner.

The cards show vampires in their royal beauty, but it doesn't just have the typical cards. The deck also includes many hybrid vampires, including angels, fairies, snakes, ghosts, demons, and werewolves. The vampire mythos is represented in each card in this deck.

The symbolisms in the cards are as diverse as the vampires. There are astrological signs, Greek and Roman gods and goddesses, and color, and more are included on each card. These cards are not cartoonish or campy like many of the other vampire decks.

In the companion guide, Ian Daniels has created a wonderful story of the secrets and desires that are within each card. There is such detail concerning colors, animals, water, moons, etc., that it would take months to really study and master the meanings of this deck.

You may purchase these cards at Llewellyn.com or on Amazon.com

~~Vampire Perfume Fangz is a great gift for Vampire Lovers~

Fangz is one of the best vampire-themed perfumes. It has been released from Wooded Ridge, a family company that has a varying stock of crafts and products, including candles and perfume.

The bottle is very feminine, reminding one of a woman that is bare-shouldered, wearing a black cape. The fragrance is described on the website as "a fragrance somewhere between the old vampire and the new. Fangz sneaks up on you with a gentle kiss of sweet, and then whispers vanilla and musk."

Here is the promotional tag for the fragrance:

"He was suddenly there, cool breath whispering close. In an instant, I sensed a story that was to take centuries to unfold...."

If this doesn't sell you on the perfume, then their promotional video will. It shows a group of young girls following the smell of the perfume to its source in the woods. It is a little long, but is creative. The video and the picture is to the right and is available via the promotional package for the company.

When you order your romantic and dangerous perfume, it comes in a clear top box with polyfill and lace, black tulle wrap and bow. The 2 oz. perfume is sold for $34.95. Hurry and get yours while supplies last and be prepared for a wonderful seduction to your senses.

To buy Fangz, or for more information, please visit the website http://fangzstory.woodedridge.com/

~Interview with Hugo Pecos, creator of The Federal Vampire and Zombie Agency ~

The Federal Vampire and Zombie Agency is an alternative history site founded by Richard Dargon. Richard created the role of Hugo Pecos as a creative outlet for all the questions that he had in regards to what if vampires and zombies were real. From these questions, he created a website that brings to life that alternative world.

In real life, Richard is a paid writer with interests in dramatic writing, screenplays, and stage plays. He also has a background in biochemistry, hence the love for science fiction.

Here is the interview that I did with Richard Dargon AKA Mr. Pecos:

Question: What is the FVZA? When did you come up with the idea?

Answer: The FVZA is the Federal Vampire and Zombie Agency. I posted the first pages of the site in the spring of 2001.

Question: How did you come up with the idea of FVZA?

Answer: It all started with a basic question: how would human history be different if vampires and zombies were real? Answering that inevitably led to a federal agency tasked with containing the undead, and that led to Dr. Hugo Pecos.

Question: Can you tell me the history of "FVZA" as you have presented it to the public?

Answer: The FVZA was formed in the years after the U.S. Civil War in response to the growing menace of vampires and zombies. The agency was ill-equipped and underfunded in its early days, but as the decades passed, it became an elite team of monster hunters. Eventually, the agency had to go undercover in response to legal issues surrounding the killing of vampires and zombies. The agency was disbanded in 1975 because it was thought that the problem was over. Some twenty-five years later, retired agent Hugo Pecos started the FVZA site to honor the agency and his fellow agents. The best part of having an eighty-five-year-old alter ego is that I don't have to make apologies for my poor web design skills! It makes sense in the context of the site.

Question: How has the FVZA been received in the "real" world?

Answer: There has been an interesting set of reactions to the site. I've heard from would-be vampires and would-be hunters. I've heard some crackpot theories. One person even complained about his tax dollars going to waste funding such an agency.

Question: I read Hugo Pecos' biography on the website. You did such a great job on intertwining fact and fiction. Can you tell me about how it came about?

Answer: It was a matter of going back in time, looking at what was happening in the United States and trying to tie a man's story to those events. New Mexico is a strange state, with Roswell and the Manhattan Project, so it seemed possible that there could be vampire and zombie research going on here.

Question: Are there any books, comics, or any material that is associated with FVZA? Can you tell me about it?

Answer: The comic book had a three-issue run in 2009/2010, and the trade paperback came out in 2010. It was written by David Hine and published by Radical Comics. David used the site for background in creating his own take. Hugo Pecos is a central character in the story.

Question: How has your life changed since your created FVZA?

Answer: I have had some opportunities where I attended a few ComicCons, did some radio shows, and guest starred on MTV. I have had to turn down a couple of TV talk shows because they wanted Hugo Pecos, not me. Mostly, I learned things. I learned how to run a web site and how to use the Internet to create a palpable alternate history. I learned I should have registered the domain FVZA.com in addition to FVZA.org. I hope to do something like this again, but in a different realm of science fiction. Hopefully, something that won't become so overcrowded.

Question: Where do you see FVZA going in the next five to ten years?

Answer: In 2009, the FVZA site was optioned by a movie production company called Contrafilm. They wanted to develop it as a comic book and then use the site and the books to generate interest from a movie studio. They have arrangements with Warner Brothers and New Line. The comic book is finished and things are in the works on the movie front, but nothing definite yet. I believe it would be the first time a website was developed into a comic book and then a movie. We'll see. I don't have any control over the direction it takes, but I hope it's something different than what's out there. The vampire and zombie field has gotten crowded in just the ten years since the site debuted.

You can find more information at the website www.fvza.org.

~~~VAMPIRES ON THE WEB~~~

There are millions of vampire websites on the internet. In the following list, you will find sites that have been voted as the most entertaining and informative. At time of publishing, all sites have been updated recently and still very active. The types of websites range from blogs to news and webisodes.

~~Vampire Websisodes~~

- Becoming Human – www.becominghuman.com
- Blood and Bone China- www.bloodandbonechina.com
- Firefly's Kiss – www.bitemereallyhard.com
- I am Tim: A Monster of a Documentary – www.hisnameistim.com
- Stake This – www.stakethis.com
- Suck and Moan – www.suckandmoan.com
- The Dead Hour – www.thedeadhour.com
- The Lawson Vampire – www.jonfmerz.net
- Transitions – www.transitionstheseries.com
- Vampire Mob- www.vampiremon.com
- Vampire News Network – coming Fall 2014
- Vampires 2012 Reality Show – www.vampirestheshow.com

~~Vampire Websites~~

- A Blood Moon – bitten2ice.com
- Amy Mah – amymah.com
- Andrea Dead Scoyoe – advanscoyoc.blogspot.com

- Anne Rice's Vampire Lestat Club – vampireleststfanclub.com
- Artisfactstore- www.artisfactstore.com
- Atlanta Vampire Alliance- www.atlantavampirealliance.com
- Bela Lugosi – www.belalugosi.com
- Bite Me Really Hard- www.bitemereallyhard.com
- Black Gate- www.blackgate.com
- Bloodlit Radio – www.bloodlitradio.com
- Bloody Good Vampires- www.bloodygoodvampires.blogspot.com
- Crazy Duck Press – www.crazyduckpress.com
- Dread Central – www.dreadcentral.com
- Drink Deeply and Dream – www.drinkdeeplyanddream.com
- Fang-tastic Books – www.fang-tasticbooks.blogspot.com
- Father Sebastian – www.fathersebastian.com
- FEARnet- www.fearnet.com
- Federal Vampire and Zombie Association- www.fvza.org
- Get Fanged - getfanged.com
- Horror Writer's Association – horror.org
- House Kheperu - kheperu.org
- Infernal Dreams- infernaldreams.net
- Les Vampires- lesvampires.org
- Living Dead Media – livingdeadmedia.com
- Loves Vampires - lovevampires.com
- Monstropedia - monstropedia.org/index.php?title=Vampire
- NEAR Paranormal – www.nearparanormal.com

- Paranormal Encounters Network – www.paraencountersnetwork.com
- Psychic Vampire – www.psychicvampire.org
- Real Vampire News for the Vampire Community – www.realvampirenews.com
- Sanguinarium – www.sanguinarium.net
- Shadow Lore- www.shadowlore.net
- Suburban Vampire - suburbanvampire.blogspot.com
- Taliesin Meets the Vampire – www.taliesinttlg.blogspot.com
- Temple of the Vampire – www.vampiretemple.com
- The Amateur Vampirologist - thevampirologist.blogspot.com.au/
- The Daily Fang- www.thedailyfang.blogspot.com
- The Dead Hour – www.thedeadhour.com
- The Gothic Catwalk – www.thegothiccatwalk.co.uk
- The Monster Channel- www.roktv.com
- The Monster Librarian – monsterlibrarian.com
- The Ringmaster's Realm - theringmastersrealm.blogspot.com
- The Vampire Source- thevampiresource.com
- The World Through Night Tinted Glasses - zahirblue.blogspot.com
- True Blood Examiner - examiner.com/true-blood-in-national/bertena-varney
- Vampire Almanac- www.vampirealmanac.com
- Vampire Art – coolest-vampire-art-gallery.com
- Vamp Culture – www.vampculture.com
- Vampire Examiner - examiner.com/vampire-in-national/bertena-varney
- Vampire Mob - vampiremob.com

- Vampire Mythology Hotspots of the Paranormal hotspotsz.com/Vampire_mythology_(Article-17806).html
- Vampire Rave - vampirerave.com
- Vampire Sexual Secrets- vampiresexualsecrets.com
- Vampire Vineyards - vampirevineyards.com
- Vampire Vixens - vampire-vixens.com
- Vampire Wear- vampirewear.com
- Vampires – www.vampires.com
- Vamplets Vampire Babies – www.vamplets.com
- Vampyres Only – www.vampyres.ca
- Vampireologist – www.Vamped.com

~~Vampire News Network is Coming Soon ~~

Vampire News Network is an alternative news program for the night breed. Inspired by the nonfiction book series by Stavros and Bertena Varney, M.A., M.Ed, *Vampire News* provides news, information, weather, and interviews from the horror, sci-fi, fantasy, gaming, comic book, and cos play genres.

After three years of a huge success of the book and Stavros' popularity as a fangsmith, fans have asked that we combine these talents into a new online television show titled, *Vampire News Network.* The *VNN* is planning on having a weekly news shows with authors, artists, and stories about vampires in the news at that time.

Currently, the *Vampire News Network* is building its set in Kansas City, MO and shooting its first two episodes as pilots in a pitch for several online web channels. They are hoping that the continued support and interest in *VNN* and its books, artists, and online program aids them in getting the show online in a regular, weekly platform!

For more information about submitting to the *Vampire News* Books, the yearly anthology of vampire news or to help sponsor or become a part of *Vampire News Network,* simply visit the website at www.crazyduckpress.com. Trust me; you will be amazed.

~~~VAMPIRES IN EDUCATION~~~

For centuries, people have studied the legend of the vampire. In earlier times, it was the church and philosophers that would research what many would call vampires and write books about what they found. Since modern times have come around, we are still researching the vampire to learn more about the creature in history, mythology, film, and literature. In this section, you will find a list of a few academics that have spent most of their studies dealing with the vampire. Each have written books and lectured on the subject. Their websites are listed.

The essay in this section is very personal to me, as it is my story of how I came to study vampires.

~~Vampire Academic Specialists~~

- Dom Augustin Calmet - http://en.wikipedia.org/wiki/Antoine_Augustin_Calmet
- Leo Allatius - http://en.wikipedia.org/wiki/Leo_Allatius
- Tina Rath - http://www.academicvampire.co.uk/
- Katherine Ramsland - www.katherineramsland.com
- J. Gordon Melton - http://en.wikipedia.org/wiki/J._Gordon_Melton
- Bertena Varney – http://www.bertena.com

~~Academic and Research Associations~~

- American Culture Association - pcaaca.org/
- Pop Culture Association - pcaaca.org/
- The Dracula Society - thedraculasociety.org.uk
- The Whedon Studies Association – slayageonline.com
- Transylvanian Society of Dracula - blooferland.com/tsd.html
- Vampire Empire- http://wiki2.benecke.com/index.php?title=The_Vampire_Empire

~~Academic Studies Websites~~

- European Vampire Research www.shroudeater.com
- Philosophical Studies of Buffy the Vampire Slayer and Angel the Series http://www.atpobtvs.com/
- Slayage www.slayageonline.com - graduate and professional studies papers dealing with the academic study of the world of Joss Whedon- *Buffy the Vampire Slayer* and *Angel*.
- Watcher Junior www.watcherjunior.tv An online journal of undergraduate collection of papers on the world of Joss Whedon.
- Whedon Studies Association http://slayageonline.com/WSA.htm This is an academic website for students and professor to discuss all of Joss Whedon's creations including *Buffy the Vampire Slayer* and *Angel*.

~~Documentaries~~

- *A Day with a Vampire*. 2010. Paranormal TV
- *Across the Forest*. 2012. www.acrosstheforrest.com
- *Dracula: The Vampire and The Voivode* 2008
- *Monster Quest: Vampires in America*. 2007. History Channel
- *Secret Lives of Women- The Occult*. 2008. WETV
- *The Secret Life of Vampires*. 2005. A&E
- *Vampire Forensics*. 2010. National Geographic
- *Vampire Secrets*. 2006. History Channel
- *Vampires: Why the Bite*. 2010

~~10 Uses of Academic Symbolism for Vampires in Pop Culture Studies~~

- Feminism and the Strength of Modern Female Characters
- Syphilis, AIDS/HIV and other diseases
- Homosexuality
- Xenophobia
- Addiction
- Obsession with youth/immortality
- Eroticism
- Escapism
- Fear of science and technology
- Acting out Violent Desires

~List of Nonfiction Books~

- *A Girls' Guide to Vampires* by Barb Karg
- *Allure of the Vampire: Our Sexual Attraction to the Undead* by Corvis Nocturnum
- *American Vampires* by Norine Drresser
- *Buffy Goes Dark* edited by Lynne Y. Edwards, Elizabeth Rambo, and James B. South
- *Count Dracula Goes to the Movies* by Lindon W. Joslin
- *DeGraecorum* by Lee Allatius (1645)
- *Dracula Unbound* by Brian Aldiss
- *Dracula: Prince of Many Faces* by Radu Florescu and Raymond T. McNally
- *Embracing the Darkness: Understanding Dark Subcultures* by Michelle Belanger
- *House of Kheperu Archives* by Michelle Belanger
- *In Search of Dracula* by Raymond T. McNally and Radu Florescu
- *On the Truths Contained in Popular Superstitions* (1851) by Herbert Mayo
- *Posthumous Humanity* 1887 by Adolphe d'Assier
- *Reflections on Dracula* by Elizabeth Miller
- *Sacred Hunger* by Michelle Belanger
- *Stage Blood* by Roxana Stuart
- *Striking a Chord: A Look at Harry Potter, Twilight and The Hunger Games* by D. MacDowell Blue
- *Sundays with Vlad* by Paul Bibeau
- *The Aesthetics of Culture in Buffy the Vampire Slayer* by Matthew Pateman
- *The Blood Countess* by Andrei Codresceu
- *The Complete Idiots Guide to Vampires* by Jay Stevenson

- *The Dead Travel Fast* by Eric Nuzum
- *The Dissertation on the Vampire* by Johann Zopfu and Francis von Dalen 1733
- *The Dracula Book* by Donald Glut
- *The Everything Vampire Book* by Barbara Karg, Arjean Spaite and Rick Sutherland
- *The Golden Age* by Apuleius
- *The Legend and Romance of the Vampire* by Derek Hall
- *The Legends of Blood: the Vampire History and Myth* by Wayne Bartlett and Plavia Idiceamu
- *The Psychic Vampire Codex* by Michelle Belanger
- *The Romance of Dracula on Celluloid* by Charles Butler
- *The Vampire Almanac* by Father Sebastian
- *The Vampire Book: The Encyclopedia of the Undead* by J. Gordon Melton
- *The Vampire Book: the Legends, Lore and the Allure* by Sally Regan
- *The Vampire Encyclopedia from A to Z* by Matthew Bunson
- *The Vampire Gallery* by J. Gordon Melton
- *The Vampire Hunters Handbook* by Erin Slonaker
- *The Vampire in the 19th Century English Literature* edited by Leonard G. Heldreth and Mary Phary
- *The Vampire Ritual Book* by Michelle Belanger
- *The Vampire Survival Guide* by Scott Bowen
- *The Vampires of History* by Donald Glut
- *Vampire Lovers* by Gavin Baddeley
- *Vampire News: Tasty Bits to Sink Your Fangs Into* by Stavros and Bertena Varney
- *Vampire: His Kith and Kin* by Montague Summers
- *Vampires* by Bob Curran

- *Vampires* by Joules Taylor
- *Vampires Everywhere: The Rise of the Movie Undead* by Charles E. Butler
- *Vampires From Dracula to Twilight* by Charlotte Montague
- *Vampires in their Own Words* by Michelle Belanger
- *Vampires: A Blood Thirsty History in Art and Literature* by Diana Phillips-Summers
- *Vampires: The Final Hunt* by Charles E. Butler
- *Vampires: Under the Hammer* by Charles E. Butler
- *Walking the Twilight Path: A Gothic Book of the Dead* by Michelle Belanger

∿ It's Time to go to School and Study...Vampires!∿

Study vampires? What? That must be a joke? Do you think you are a vampire? Wow, where do you get something like that... a crackerjack box?

These are all questions and sometimes not-too-nice comments that I receive when I tell people that I research and write about vampires. They look at me as if I am a freak and my education a joke. When I try to defend myself and tell them my degrees, I lose credibility. At times, it has even resulted in me losing jobs or not getting hired when employers do a Google search on me. But, if you are willing and ready to learn, I can share with you my journey to studying vampires.

First, my background and how I came to study vampires: I have multiple degrees. The first is a Bachelor's of Arts in Social Science and Education with an emphasis in sociology, history, and government and a minor in geography and economics. During that study, I chose several topics to focus on when I had freedom of projects and classes. These ranged from History of Folklore, where I studied Vampire Folklore, to deviant subcultures, where I studied vampire lifestylers. I had to be careful because this was from 1989-1993 and there was and still is a huge stigma about anything Goth or dark or relating to vampires.

After successfully completing my bachelor's, I then pursued a Master's in Sociology and Criminology, where I studied juvenile delinquency and deviant subcultures. During this time, vampires, Goths, and the like were considered deviant and to show any sign of "liking" this would have destroyed my position as a Graduate Assistant. So, I pursued those from a very strict academic point of view.

After graduation, I trotted off to the real world of teaching high school and gained an adjunct teaching position at Eastern Kentucky University. While there, I spoke with coworkers who were pursuing their doctoral degrees. I knew that I had to finish my Master's in Education because the wonderful state of Kentucky requires it to maintain a teaching certification in that state. So I completed my educational component, but was left with my subject component. I had taken all the graduate classes that they had offered in social science and I was told that there were no more classes to take, but that I still had credits to complete in order to graduate.

I began discussing and researching my options when I found that, in larger universities, there were graduate studies in pop culture and several academic associations dealing with the study of things such as cartoons, comic books, and television shows. The topics were too numerous to count. But, I did find one I liked – vampires.

The most popular academic study of vampires at the time dealt specifically with one of my favorite television shows, *Buffy the Vampire Slayer*. The Whedon Studies Association is a group of professors and students who study the work of Joss Whedon, which includes *Angel* and *Buffy*. They have an online journal, yearly convention, and a great website that helps those who want to study this subject to look at it through feminist, historical, sociological, and psychological viewpoints.

So I gathered up my list of academic programs and academic research, created an outline for a class, and took it to my advisor at Morehead State University. She agreed to allow me to design the class topic, do the research, and write my final paper on vampires! I was so excited! I had always hated to write, but for the first time in my life, I knew I was going to love to write on this topic.

I spent the semester researching and writing and searching for the lure of the vampire. When I finished the class, I knew that I wanted to continue this study and to continue writing about this wonderful creature of the night. After graduation, I joined several academic organizations to continue my academic study on vampires.

I still receive the weird looks and comments, but the study of the Lure of the Vampire is real. It is a legitimate academic topic and is becoming a very popular one in college classrooms, ranging from Ohio to Louisiana, England, and Canada. There are numerous approved classes and they are always overloaded.

Vampire studies can be found under several degree areas: sociology, psychology, philosophy, creative writing, literature studies, history, art, pop culture, and media studies. Simply talk to your counselor about independent study or any other degree that is relative to these above. Many graduates have become writers or involved in the media as a result of their interest in the vampires.

But, for now, vampires are slowly becoming a credible academic study for many who find creative ways to either include the vampire in their classes or have been as lucky as I have with finding a very supportive professor.

~~~VAMPIRES IN REAL LIFE~~~

In this section, we are going to discuss vampires who live their lives as vampires, whether it is a need for blood, energy, or other reasons. These "vampire" names are included with permission either from the person or the group in which they are a member. If you decide to contact them, please do so with respect and do not threaten or antagonize them. They are willing to discuss their lifestyle and should not be persecuted for it.

Remember that many live by the teachings of The Black Veil, which lays out rules for behavior, donors, communities, discretion, diversity, control, and respect for elders. They are a very respectful subculture, so please show the same respect to them. Remember: Light and Love to all.

~~Types of Human Living Vampires~~

- Astral Vampires are people who use astral projection to feed on the living by penetrating the aura and physical body. They feed off the energy of the other person.
- Auto erotic or Blood Fetish Vampires are people who enjoy drinking their own blood for sexual pleasure. The blood may come by an accidental cut or by self-mutilation.
- Clinical Vampirism, also known as Reinfield's Syndrome, has not been accepted by the DSM, but has been referenced by psychiatrists. It is very rare and

- usually occurs in males. They have an obsession to drink blood expressed as a physical need. They usually do not label themselves vampires. They usually drink their own blood first and then others' later. It is not an accepted diagnosis by medical groups.
- Elemental Vampires are people who believe that they can feed off natural phenomena such as thunderstorms, lightning, hurricanes, and other natural phenomena. They can also feed off the earth and crystals. This feeding or energy surge provides them with the energy to live and to function daily.
- Lifestylers are people who enjoy dressing up as a vampire either in Victorian or Goth clothing. They may wear contacts, fangs, or other costume pieces. They are usually only attracted to the vampire lore.
- Psychic, Pranic, Energy, or Psi Vampires are people who believe that they can feed off of the energy of others. Many times, these persons are harmless and will only "drink from your life force" after asking your permission. But, there are times when those that consider themselves psychic vampires "feed off" of you without your permission. This is strictly not allowed in the vampire community and is not encouraged. Psychic vampires may also be people who are not aware that they feed off of energy. Have you met anyone who just drains your energy, or who is always negative? Well, these people feed off of whatever you are giving them, whether it's empathy or just a listening ear. These people are not ones that live the lifestyle, but have the same effect on people as a psychic vampire except that the lifestylers ask permission first before they feed from your energy.

- Sanguanarians are people who believe that they must consume small amounts of blood in order to survive. They have regular consenting healthy donors that donate blood for them to fulfill a physical need, not a sexual need. Those with a general blood fetish are attracted to the sight, smell, and taste of blood in general. Many times, this represents an emotional hunger for attachments.
- Tantric, Sexual, or Sympathetic Vampires are people who believe that they feed on sexual energy that comes through a state of euphoria which uses the Hindu practice of Tantra, a sort of meditational state.

~~10 Websites used by those that label themselves "Vampire"~~

These websites are for those that choose the lifestyle. When visiting them, please remember to treat the members and the site with respect. No harassing or threatening posts, please.

- Dark Sites www.darksites.com
- Darkness Embraced www.darknessembraced.com
- Psychic Vampires http://psychicvampire.org/index.htm
- Sanguinarius www.sanguinarius.org
- Vampire Freaks www.vampirefreaks.com
- Vampire Realm of Darkness www.vampires.nu
- Vampire Social www.vampiresocial.com
- Vampires http://vampirewebsite.net
- New Orleans Vampire Association - http://www.neworleansvampireassociation.org/

~Interview with a Vampire - Vlad the Gothic Magician~

On Halloween 2005, I was accepted as a presenter at The Witching Hour: a Harry Potter Symposium in Salem, Massachusetts. Harry Potter has always been an interest of mine, but vampires were always my favorite. While in Salem, I was shocked and excited when I met Vlad, the Gothic Vampire Magician. I was awestruck! When he told me that he was doing a show that evening in Salem, I was there first! I went and I absolutely LOVED his show. It was not just a magic show, but a theatrical performance. Without giving too much away, I can say that the show mesmerized the audience. The unique twist with traditional vampire stories and modern magic was perfect.

I later found out that being a vampire was not just part of his show, but a part of his life. When approached about the request to allow me to interview him about both his business and his life, he was very gracious. I want to thank him here as well as thank him for use of his image on the cover of the book.

Here is the interview:

Question: When did you develop the concept of the Gothic Magician?

Answer: I started in magic in 1985. I was brought into it through being a special affects artist at Kevin McCurdy's Haunted Mansion in Wappingers Falls, NY. Kevin had previously been a magician and suggested that it might be a road I would enjoy investigating. At the time, I had never thought of magic as a career because there was not much known about "Magic organizations." So, I asked him, "Don't you have to be born into Magic, or don't they come in the middle of the night and bring you to the sacred grove by candlelight?" He replied, "No, you just have to go to meetings." This was my first magical disappointment.

Question: Please tell me about how you came up with the idea of Vlad the Gothic Magician. Where did you get the ideas for the show?

Answer: When Kevin suggested Magic as a career, I sought inspiration from the local Magicians. Most did not understand what I was trying to bring across to the audience, because I had no desire to do birthday parties or the like. I was then introduced to Jeff McBride (http://www.mcbridemagic.com), who was trying to create something called Mystery School. The purpose was to intertwine stage magicians and ceremonial magicians in a magical space to explore magic's roots. It began in 1992 and is still around today. This is where I created Gothic Magic. My first incarnation was to be sort of a Rod Serling death personified character. I then realized that I had to incorporate my vampiric self and magical self with my love of the horror genre. Vlad the Gothic Magician was born.

Question: To what do you attribute your success?

Answer: I try and give people an experience they won't get anywhere else. I bring them the same theatrical experience that a good movie or play does. There is humor, sadness, tension, romance, and more. I don't think most Magic performances consider involving all the senses of sight, sound, smell, and touch. I want to take my audience on a roller coaster ride to death's door, beyond, and then back.

Question: Where have you performed and which is the most interesting, unusual, or fun performance?

Answer: Wow! That could be an essay in itself. Well, that includes a number of the Endless Night Vampire balls in NYC, the Vampire Balls in Salem, MA, the NY Renaissance Faire, Fright Kingdom, House of the Living Dead, Life & Death in Salem, and really too many to name here. Just take a peek at my website for a more complete list. But, I have to say that one of the coolest events that I have participated in was performing for MGM Studios and Clive Barker at the VIP Party at the premiere of Lord of Illusions at Webster Hall in NYC.

Question: I understand that there is an entire subculture or world of magic. Can you discuss the world of magic - like professional organizations, etc.?

Answer: The two largest Magic organizations are S.A.M which is The Society of American Magicians. S.A. is for those over eighteen and we have a younger version named S.Y.M that stands for the Society of Young Magicians. There is an international organization called I.B.M or the International Brotherhood of Magicians.

Smaller interest groups include The Academy of Magical Arts (The Magic Castle), The Magic Circle (London), and The Inner Circle of Bizarre Magick that caters to Bizarre, Storyteller, Mystery, Séance performers. The existence of the groups can be spoken of and frequently the events they have can also be attended by non-magicians, but the lectures or private workshop can only be attended by members or practitioners of the arts.

Question: Do you have any suggestions for anyone who is interested in getting into this line of work?

Answer: Study acting and improvisational skills. These will be the most valuable in your career as the methods of magic. If a presentation is not entertaining and engaging, it becomes a mere puzzle. Be original; if you seek to copy someone, it will show. You can be inspired, but don't go overboard. If you copy someone still alive, why would someone hire you when they can book the original?

Question: What are the stories that you use in your show? How did you come up with these stories?

Answer: I use references to Poe in my Buried Alive piece, Countess Elizabeth Bathory, legends involving death, Jekyll and Hyde, and more. The venue or theme of the show inspires me to create some pieces; sometimes, the prop or the item speaks to me.

Question: How do magic and vampires intertwine?

Answer: Well, a lot of myths claim sorcerers and witches become vampires. If we look into that claim, they both control or manipulate the elements, they both have longevity or immortality, and they both hold secrets. My concept for my character or persona was if I actually had to live forever, what would I do to entertain myself? I found that I would do things like magic that were natural to me, but unbelievable to mortals. But all the hypnosis, magic, etc. in that role can be claimed to be all just an illusion so as to conceal my identity.

Question: Do you consider yourself a vampire other than your magician persona?

Answer: Yes, I am a living vampire, though not a mythical one.

Question: Can you tell what a living vampire is and what it means to you?

Answer: A living vampire does not delude themselves by believing that they can morph into a wolf or bat, change into mist, live forever, or control the weather. We understand the inherent concepts of the vampire and through either sanguine or pranic (drawing of energy), manipulate energy for ourselves (not that different in concept than Tantra or Reiki).

Questions: Do you feel that this helps you in your magic shows?

Answer: I think anytime you honor, understand, and pay tribute to magic, it shows in your performance, I also believe that if the words you speak come from your heart, with your passion within them, people can feel it.

Question: How do the audiences react?

Answer: Well, I hope, I see and feel the range of their emotions and respond to them. If a piece gets no reaction, no matter how much I may love it, it is cut. It does no good to keep it. Otherwise, it would be like serving a dish that the only person that likes it is the chef.

Question: Is there a connection between the role you play as a magician and your "real life"?

Answer: I personally don't follow any organized religion. I understand that energy exists and I respect the universe. But I feel that if I live my life to the best of my abilities, no one has the right to judge me. I also know that the energy of the universe can be tuned into, so yes, according to most mystic paths, I do indeed lead a magical life.

Question: Can you tell me anything about that "world" or "life" of a living vampire?

Answer: I'm an Elder in the Society Nocturnus of Gotham. It used to be the Sanguinarium. In New York City, there are two courts named Lazarus and Nocturnus respectively. The courts are presided over by a Regent who is voted in by the Citizens, which include elders, ronins, calmae. Under the regent are the individual Houses that are divided into clutches or covens. Within these courts are sergeant-at-arms and sometimes sheriffs as the community self-polices to try and avert drama from coming down on all for the mistakes of one.

Question: What else have you done in theater or on television?

Answers: I was in *Tales from the Black Veil* and *The Gotham Chronicles*, an Off Broadway play. As well as *Marat Sade* and *Grandma Sylvia's Funeral* and an *Inspector Call*.

Films include *Toxic Avenger 4: Citizen Toxie*, where I was an extra in several scenes.

Television credits are: (CBC) *Man Alive Mystery School Documentary*, (TLC) *Grand Illusions: The Story of Magic*, (DSC) *Great Books: Dracula* and a pilot we did called *Strange Attractors*.

Question: Can you tell me how you came about to be in the book – *Sundays with Vlad*?

Answer: That was such a great honor. *Sundays with Vlad* is an investigation into the world's fascination with the vampire as an iconic image. When the author was doing research, I was found because I was one of very few vampire magicians and the only one named Vlad.

Question: Are there any videos or movies that you would like to link to this interview?

Answer: Yes. Here is the Strange Attractors YouTube clip: http://www.youtube.com/watch?v=4m5yWHroCuI

As well as my 2009 performance in Salem, MA: https://www.facebook.com/video/video.php?v=1743137296238

Question: What is your connection with Festival of the Dead? What roles do you play?

Answer: I was crowned King of the New England Vampires by Shawn Poirier at one of the first Vampire Balls and have been involved either as host or performer ever since. Information can be found at www.festvialofthedead.com

Question: How can we get more information about Vlad and the Gothic Magician?

Answer: My website is www.GothicMagic.com. I have recently moved to North Carolina to help with family and am doing theater and other work there, but my website is still the best way to get in touch with me.

Thank you again, Vlad, for agreeing to speak with me about not only your stage life, but your personal life as well. And thank you for all that you have done to support me in this endeavor.

I would also like to thank you for allowing me to use your image as the first edition book cover. I think that it just adds to the lure of the vampire.

~Interview with the Vampiric Council of New England~

In the previous interview, Vlad mentioned covens of vampires in New York City. By his referral I contacted the coven as a group and requested an interview. They graciously agreed and here is what I discovered about the Vampiric Council of New England.

Question: I guess the first question would be what is the Vampiric Council of New England?

Answer: The Vampiric Council of New England is a group in which the members are made up of vampires, like-minded individuals and otherkin seeking each other.

Question: Who does the Vampiric Council consist of and what type of person would be interested in joining?

Answer: Those interested in joining would have experienced an awakening, the realization of who and what they are. Our council members consist simply of the founder, Dimitri, Elders, Vlad, and Blackwolf. It also includes members that have awakened unto themselves and desire the company of those with similar interests as well as learning and understanding the modern vampiric culture.

Question: Are the members from a certain demographic group such as age, social economic status, or geographic area?

Answer: The group accepts anyone over the age of eighteen years old that would like to seek guidance and support no matter their religion, dress, status, or sexual preference.

Question: What would you want the world to know about the Council?

Answer: Some of the council members were there at the start of THE SOCIETY NOCTURNUS OF GOTHAM, NY. This was the beginning of The Black Veil, the "13 rules" written for the vampire community. The members of Vampiric Council of New England have come together to form a bond stronger than mere friendship.

Question: Can you explain for us what the Black Veil is?

Answer: The Black Veil was created originally to protect the vampire community. It was written to keep away violence. The principles in the Black Veil are common sense values that keep us safe, thrive, and give us freedom in the mundane world. It has been modified a few times since then with a few different versions. These changes were made to keep up with the changing of society in the vampiric world.

Question: What does it mean or entail to be a "vampire"?

Answer: Ask a hundred vampires and get a hundred answers. Being labeled as such is where most would disagree. Some would say the troubles labeling themselves have caused is a disadvantage while others would give the advantages of being labeled a vampire is desirable. Everyone is different because it is the way each of us would view a situation. No two vampires are the same. Vampires know they are different from others and, after "awakening," they realize that this is what they are "labeled as." Some may do research via internet to help them figure it out or use other resources. Once one accepts themselves as such, they should learn all that they possibly can and have respect and responsibility.

Question: What are some problems that you think that your group may face in the mainstream?

Answer: The problems that the group may face are those that do not understand, may follow the mythical and/or movie genre. Another problem is that they would believe that vampires are evil.

Question: Do you receive any support in the community?

Answer: We have received support from local businesses and other head organizers and Elders of other various groups. They are all willing to help us continue to grow in New England.

Question: Are there links or additional material like pictures, videos that you would be willing to share?

Answer: You can find us on Facebook at:

http://www.facebook.com/home.php#!/pages/Vampiric_Counc il_of_New_England/177767997487 as well as Meetup.com

I would like to thank the members of the Vampiric Council of New England for taking time out to do this interview. They have been very helpful in allowing us to learn more about their organization. The interview was very enlightening and we greatly appreciate their honesty and time.

~Interview with a Vampire Priestess – Audrey Koogler~

Vampire Priestess? Yes, you read the title correctly. I have been corresponding with Audrey for a few months now and found her lifestyle very interesting and unique, in my experience. Here is her interview. Hope you enjoy it as much as I do.

Question: Audrey, please tell us about yourself and your interests.

Answer: My name is Audrey; yes, that is my name. I did have a "vampire" name at one point, but I dispensed with it. Why have a pseudonym for who I am? I am a solitary vampire in that I currently have no "coven" or other recognized vampire official affiliation. I am building my own Temple, but it is not exclusively for vampires, but for all darkly inclined creatures. My titles are Shaman, Minister, and Teacher. My associates come up with more, but those take in most of what I do!

Question: I have asked this question to everyone and am curious as to how you define what a vampire is?

Answer: I am sure by now you have discovered there are about as many definitions and forms of vampire as there are vampires! I take each person for their own story and experience. Unfortunately, there are always those who say this is not a vampire or this is. The same is true with Goths. I believe that whether your first introduction to what you will become is from literature, art, movies, ads, or even a cereal box, there is no wrong way to come into yourself. So what is a vampire? That depends on the vampire!

Question: Please tell us about your beliefs as well as your personal and professional responsibilities?

Answer: I call myself a Dark Practitioner. I am ordained through the Universal Life Church as a minister; I can perform legal weddings as well as handfastings, funerals, blessings, naming, etc. I teach about the metaphysical Path of Darkness and Shadows. My intent is to teach people to understand the Shadow Self and the darker parts of our nature and to be able to embrace and work with these, making us whole beings. I also teach tarot reading and run the occasional Goddess workshop. I also function as a counselor for many. I believe it is my responsibility to teach people about the Darkness and Shadow, which is part of us all, to lead them to a better understanding and acceptance of this side of nature.

Question: Where are some places that you socialize?

Answer: I am Gothic, a Romanti-goth, to be specific. Not all vampires are Goths and certainly not all Goths are vampires! There are far too many forms of the Gothic culture out there! I am a vampire who happens to be a Goth. I therefore love to go to Goth clubs and events. I also have a group of friends who love to gather for movie nights and themed parties as well as many other types of events. Shakespeare in the Park every year! As a vampire, I am accepted among my friends and family for who and what I am. I know that makes me very lucky. I often try to seek out other vampires, but our secretive nature makes that a challenge. Not to mention, there are many posers and pretenders out there!

Question: When did you decide or discover that you were a vampire?

Answer: I have heard many vampires refer to theirs as an "Awakening." I refer to myself as "coming out of the coffin." It wasn't a sudden change for me, similar to many gay and transgender people; I have always had a feeling that I was not quite all me, that I was somehow masquerading. I identified strongly with the vampires I saw in movies and read in fiction to one degree or another. It was a dawning realization from very early on, around seven or so, that this is what I am and always have been. The most obvious aspects of my state are: My skin lacks the pigment to protect me from the sun. I do not tan at all; without extreme measures of protection from direct sunlight, I badly burn (ten minutes or less), then blister (fifteen to twenty minutes), then become ill and need hospitalization (anything over thirty to forty minutes). I wear the highest SPF I can find and am covered with a sun-resistant fabric that covers my hands, closes at the neck and wear a large-brimmed hat whenever I must go out into the sun.

I need very rare, red meat; other forms of protein do not sustain me. Yes, I consume blood, but that comes in many forms. The most common form is black pudding; a Gaelic blood sausage, which is the best food form of sustenance. Rare red meat is the next best. I do get weak and listless without these. I did try lean meats at one point in my life (I am a bodybuilder by hobby), chicken, fish, etc. I kept getting weaker and this was part of the confirmation to me that this is what I am and not just in my mind. There are times when arrangements can be made with willing, clean, consenting donors, but in recent times, this is increasingly difficult. I cannot speak to how the different vampire communities address this; I can only speak for myself.

Question: How do other people react to you? Do you assimilate into society for a mundane job or do you portray yourself all the time? May I ask what you do for a living?

Answer: I am myself at all times (though I do not usually wear the contacts at home); anything else would be a costume. I would feel like I am masquerading. I have held full and part-time jobs here and there, but I make my living as an artist, a teacher, and a minister. I fully believe you should be yourself and then find a way to make a living that you can live with.

Question: Are there any positive stories that you would like to share with us?

Answer: I was in a seasonal Halloween store, and I heard a little girl asking her father "Daddy, do you think we will see any vampires?" As her father was answering with the typical "…well, I don't know…" she turned the corner and walked right into me. She lit up with a huge smile and went "Daddy, look!" I was able to gently answer a few questions (child-safe answers, of course) and talk with her a little. She was one very happy seven-year-old!

Also, when my friends had their little baby girl, they asked me to be her godmother. The mom (J) told me that she thought I would be a strong influence, and an excellent example of how empowering it is to be true to yourself and your own self-expression. I was deeply honored.

Another involves my goddaughter's next older brother (S). A mutual friend often has movie parties, and sometimes these are family friendly so J and her husband bring their three kids. Both of my goddaughter's older brothers are quite fond of me, often rushing to greet me before I even get to the apartment door! That night's movies were *20,000 Leagues under the Sea* and *The League of Extraordinary Gentlemen*. The kids were all out in the main room for the first movie. S sat on my lap during most of the movie, asking a constant stream of questions about everything (he is seven). After a while, he looked up at me and asked, "What DO vampires eat?" I told him "Little boys who ask too many questions." His response: "Oh, stop." Priceless.

I have yet to meet a child that is afraid of me, other than those who are generally shy. Though sometimes the shy ones talk to me faster!

Question: Are there any negative stories that you would like to share with us?

Answer: It is hard to really say anything truly negative has happened. It is true that there are those who feel they must say something rude or inane, but I see this as a reflection of their own fears. Most people are so desperately afraid of the disapproval of others that they dull themselves and hide their true tastes and desires. The negative comments of others honestly do not bother me. I was very surprised by this at first. I am by nature a shy person and was always hypersensitive about the negative reactions of others. I believe it is because I am ridiculously happy with what I see in the mirror. (Yes, vampires do have a reflection! Some of us are very vain and would die without a mirror!) I wish there was a way to tell people the thing you fear the most is what will set you free.

Question: What else would you like for us to know about you?

Answer: I believe that we all begin our lives masquerading. That we begin from the first understanding to put on masks to please those around us; parents first, then teachers, classmates, etc., until we are being smothered in a many-layered façade that will eventually choke us. Some people break out of this mold, but most do not. I am not sure whether some people just feel the oppression more keenly or if others are more bounded by their fear; it seems to be different mixtures of both. We must all, at some point, become ourselves and question who we pretend to be and why. Those who truly love us will accept our True Selves; the rest don't really love you and have their own issues to deal with. I realize that last part sounds harsh, but the truth is, when someone is too wound up in their own damage and issues, they only perceive the world around them through a filter of fear, which makes them unable to see clearly. It is not you they are responding to, but the reflection of their own fears they are projecting.

I would like to add that I think that it is important for everyone to come out of hiding. It is better to be upfront with who and what you are so that we can educate people and try to end discrimination and judgments. All prejudicial behavior comes from a lack of understanding, and it is difficult to understand when you are keeping secrets. We need to work on discovering what is a physical condition, what is a mental disease, and/or what is natural about all Otherkin and avoid lumping it all into a fantasy, unhealthy obsession or mental illness.

Question: How could we get in touch with you if we have additional questions?

Answer: If anyone has any questions or wish to contact the Temple of Shadows: Vampire Ministry and Metaphysics of the Dark, they can e-mail me at TempleofShadowsMinistry@gmail.com. There is also a Temple of Shadows Facebook page.

~~~ABOUT THE AUTHOR~~~

Well, I was told that it is customary to create an "About the Author" section for my book. Well, if you are to learn about me, then it has to start at the beginning- with my name. So, many times I get asked – wow, is that your real last name? Well, yes, Varney is my real last name and true vampire fans will know the significance... how many of you have heard of a British penny dreadful titled, *Varney the Vampire: Feast of Blood*? Well, Varney is the name of the very scary vampire in this book that was published just before Stoker created Dracula. Of course, many claim, and I too would like to think, that Varney somehow influenced Stoker in his depictions of the Count. If you choose to read this book, be prepared... it is one of the worst books ever written. As was the custom at the time, authors were paid a penny a word for their works and Sir Thomas Prest, author of *Varney the Vampire*, certainly used more than his share to describe in agonizing detail. If you would like your own free copy of *Varney*, refer to the Literature section and click on or go to that link.

What attracted me to vampires?

My first memory of vampires was Count von Count from Sesame Street. I know it sounds corny, but I would get my mom to buy me Count Chocula cereal and I would eat it while watching Sesame Street, Count Duckula, and the Addams Family. As I grew older, I advanced to *Dark Shadows* reruns, *Cliffhangers*, and was even allowed to watch Bela Lugosi's original *Dracula*. I didn't know what he was about, this monster, but I had to know anything that I could about him. He was so mysterious, so mesmerizing, and also so dangerous. I loved the vampire because it was so human and I was able to identify with it. I spent the rest of my life immersed in vampire movies, books, television shows, comics – it didn't matter; I just loved this dark, brooding monster.

While in college, I turned my love of the vampire into an independent academic study. My undergraduate studies centered around the concentrations of social science and education and I purposely chose classes that would add to my growing library of vampire knowledge. I wrote a paper on folklore of the old world and focused on vampires. While pursuing my first graduate degree, I was studying sociology, criminology, and organized literary and first person research on deviant subcultures focused on vampire lifestyles and serial killers who were labeled as vampires. The final study – and the one that really made me realize that vampires were worthy, legitimate academic study – was when I finished my last masters in social science and education.

This last study was a master's paper titled, "Search for the Lure of the Vampire." This ultimately became the beginnings of this book. While researching the book, I found others who were on the same academic path. I joined the Whedon Studies Association, where graduate students and academics study the world of Joss Whedon. Their publications and work include an academic look into the world of both *Buffy* and *Angel*. After more research, I joined The Transylvanian Society of Dracula, The Dracula Society, The Vampire Empire, and The Dark Shadows Fan Club. I've found that there is a multitude of academic research and like-minded academics that love the study of the vampire as much as I. They were a true wealth of information and inspired me to keep on going with my writing.

My favorite aspects of vampires!

I love all aspects of the vampire – the dark animalistic creature, the brooding monster trying to redeem himself, the honorable leader of his country (Vlad), the seducer, and especially the aristocratic power of the vampire. But, my favorite thing to study is why we all love these creatures! Is it because we want to escape our mundane life in exchange for a more erotic lover, a knight in shining armor, immortality, or to represent the issues that we are dealing with in society at that moment- homosexuality, feminism, violence, etc.?

I find that the vampire helps me deal with things in my life. I find the creature in all points in history that I study, in the culture in which I interact and the stories that I read to escape this world. The vampire is just a mirror for culture; no matter if it was hundreds of years ago or now, it represents what we fear most at that moment.

My favorite vampire movie, television show, and book

There are way too many vampire movies to name. It all depends upon my mood. But with regard to movies, if I am in a traditional mood, it's Bram Stoker's *Dracula* or Bela Lugosi's *Dracula*. I also love *The Lost Boys*; it kept me dreaming through most of my teen years. If it were campy movies you have to include *My Best Friend's a Vampire, Transylvania 6-5000*, and *Once Bitten*. Any 80s vampire movie will keep me company. I love the idea of the vampire being so fluid. He can be a traditional monster of the night, or a silly bloodsucker the next. The vampire can be who or what you want them to be.

My favorite television shows are *Buffy, the Vampire Slayer* and *Blood Ties*. Henry Fitzroy, the vampire in *Blood Ties*, is the illegitimate son of Henry VIII, and I feel he portrays how a vampire would assimilate and live in modern society. He is not brooding and does not hate who he is. He accepts that he is a vampire and embraces his powers. He is the epitome of what I would love in a vampire.

Now, choosing my favorite books is easy – all of them. I love the classics, the young adult books, the adult romance, and the reference and cultural studies of the vampire subculture. To say that I had a favorite vampire book would not be honest. At this time I have four, six-foot bookshelves full of vampire literature.

But, I can say that my first vampire book was *Bunnicula*, a primary reading book. I read it every day until I could go back to the library and find more children's vampire books. I found a children's version of *Dracula* and realized that what I loved to sneak and watch on television was available for me to read and to escape to that world.

My vampire research

My research has taken me to look for vampiric themes, vampire related sites, stores, or even cultures in every city in which I have travelled. So far, I have researched and visited the story of the vampires and interesting sites in New Orleans, Savannah, Salem, Paris, and London. Even though I have enjoyed the pop culture items that the vampire provides, my research, as I travel to these places, has been my favorite. Meeting real life vampires, studying the history and folklore of the towns and even visiting sites that have been written about, as well as filming locations has been the most fun.

Lecturing and Appearances

I love to attend conferences of all types – Pop Culture Association, Harry Potter, gaming, Buffy, and more. It's fun to be around people who are like minded. But, most of all, I love to teach, lecture, write, read, and watch movies.

I have lectured at many conferences and conventions. These have included The Witching Hour, The ScareFest, The Sirens Convention in Vail, Co, The Metafaire, Fandom Fest, A Day of Mystical Blood Lust, Mystical Paranormal Fair, Carnegie Center of Literacy and Learning, as well as many libraries and colleges.

Writing and Research

Even though the *Lure of the Vampire* is the first book to be published, I have several of my lectures in compendiums and anthologies. These include *Vampires: Romance to Rippers: An Anthology of Tasty Stories, Vampires Romance to Rippers: An Anthology of Risqué Stories, Vampire News 2011, 2012,* and *2013* as well as The Witching Hour Compendium and The Sirens Compendium. I also helped Elizabeth Loraine write *Lillian: a Vampire's Story, Lillian: The Mask,* and *Lillian 3* by providing my role-playing character, Lillian, as the inspiration for the story. I have also supplemented my research for this book by writing the *Vampire Examiner* and *True Blood Examiner*. Examiner.com is a national online news source where writers are chosen for their expertise. My vampire articles have also appeared on Yahoo! Associated Content, AOL, and multiple blogs and websites.

What's next for me?

Well, vampires are not slowing down and neither am I! I am planning several stops in my book tour as well as lots of conferences and workshops so that I may meet others who love the vampire as much as I. I am also planning on moving more into the world of other supernatural creatures, such as fairies, angels, and dragons. But, most of all, I look forward to catching up on my reading of the wonderful vampire books that I have missed while writing my book.

I am also completing a vampirology course for others who want to learn how to study about the vampire in an academic way. The lessons would focus on each section of this book. This should be out before Halloween.

I have also returned to teaching college sociology and hope to continue with my study of the most influential monster of all time. I love my students and coworkers at Southcentral Community and Technical College

Where to find me

•Website www.bertena.com

•Twitter @tenavarney

•Facebook – http://www.facebook.com/bertena.varney

~~~A PREVIEW OF LILLIAN~~~

Character Created by Bertena Varney and Brought to life by Elizabeth Loraine

About the Author

I always knew I was supposed to write a book someday, but as my family grew, my artistic bent was fulfilled through interior design, painting, and garden design work. Now, as my son and daughter left home and I left commercial design and painting, I found I had more time on my hands for ignored creative desires.

I have been a lifelong fantasy fiction fan and, for years, devoured books that depicted vast worlds, populated by heroic characters. But a particular focus of my reading enjoyment for many, many years has been vampires and vampire lore. My passion for the subject, you could say, has spanned the "Bellas"; from portrayals of them by Bela Lugosi to books about them featuring Bella Swan.

Although I found their world exciting, filled with romance and adventure, somehow, at "The End," I always wanted to know more. Vampires, after all, we know are long lived; where had they come from, where had they been, what had they done, what had they seen? I longed to know their timeline and history.

From that curiosity and those questions, my creative side picked up a pen, a notebook, and out came The Royal Blood Chronicles. These books feature young, strong, self-reliant, intelligent, interesting woman as lead characters. No wimpy women victims allowed here.

My writing took a darker turn with the introduction of Lillian. This book followed a woman from her origins at the hand of her first love in England in the 1800's, forward to the present time. By chronicling her life as it changes through history, we are invited into her life of power, wealth, but also a life that has been empty of love.

I wrote the Phantom Lives Series from the point of view Abigail Black, a young heiress with a gift of the future and past sight. She is a rare being because her destiny leads her to being a Gate Keeper. With the help of her network of Seers and Sentinels, Abbi would care for all the earth's Gates, protecting other realms from dangerous incursions from our and other times and places.

Continue following Katrina, Lillian, and Abigail and all their friends and families. Enjoy their pasts and look forward to the exploits in their futures.

LILLIAN

Written by Elizabeth Loraine

Original Story by Bertena Varney

This book is available in print at most online retailers.

CHAPTER ONE

Lillian was born into a life of privilege in the year 1870. As the third daughter of the Queen of England's most trusted advisor, she had more freedoms than most young women her age.

She was given the finest education, trained to be the most gracious hostess, and all but ignored by her family. Her parents were much more interested in advancing the family fortunes by the correct political placement of their treasured eldest son and seeking out the best match by marriage of her older sisters, to focus any of their energy on her.

Lillian didn't mind their callous disregard; after all, it was all she'd ever known. She embraced the simplicity of her life and passed her time reading; not in the grandest libraries in all of England, but in the meadow, beneath her favorite tree. In addition to the setting being a serene surrounding for her insatiable consumption of a wide and eclectic range of subject matter, the location afforded her an undetectable vantage point for listening to young authors at the school. Often, their classroom discussions about their newest poetry, literary, or scientific offerings overflowed onto the patios occupying the side of the school adjacent to the meadow. The sounds of the students' raised voices while they defended their points of view carried easily to Lillian's vantage point.

Although she had very little interest in them, her attendance was mandatory at all the functions made necessary by the status of her family's wealth and privilege. Lillian did as her father demanded, and it was at one of these very functions that her life actually began. She had left the ballroom and was in the garden sitting out one of the English country dances.

"Lovely garden, isn't it?" the tall, dark stranger whispered.

Lillian jumped, pressing her delicate gloved hand to her chest.

"I'm sorry that I startled you. I assure you it is not the reaction I was seeking. My name is Alexander Whillenhaul."

Lillian was captivated instantly by this man. He was…beautiful. His smile made her knees weak and her stomach tighten.

She offered her hand to him. "I'm Lillian, Lillian Price."

He smiled again and bent from the waist to give her hand a gentle kiss.

From that night on, the two were inseparable evening companions who found that they shared a love of music, good literature, and the theatre. Several times a week, they attended the evening concerts, art shows, theatre, and readings offered to people of their class.

To her surprise and gratitude, he seemed truly interested in her opinions. Men her age had no desire to hear what she had to say, let alone entertain her ideas as anything more than amusing female folly.

Though she had always considered herself plain, Lillian felt beautiful in his eyes.

After several weeks of what she thought of as her "fall into paradise," she was totally and undeniably in love with Alexander. That evening, she asked shyly, "You will come to me again tomorrow night?"

"Of course; there is nowhere I'd rather be than in your company. I'd hoped that you realized that by now."

As they strolled leisurely back to her rooms, which were in the isolated east wing of her family's large manor house, Alexander seemed distracted.

"Is something wrong?"

"Nothing for you to worry about."

It was then that she first detected shadowy figures that seemed to be following them. Lillian felt the first tendrils of fear begin to rise in her breast.

"Please, don't keep things from me, Alex. If I am going to be a part of your life, I want to know everything. I feel you are in danger somehow, and, after these perfectly idyllic weeks, I could not bear to lose you now."

Alexander stopped and took her hands. He looked deeply into her eyes as he raised them to his lips.

"I love you," she heard in her mind.

She blinked and her widening eyes caused Alexander to smile.

"I will tell you all very soon. Now we must get you home; it's almost dawn."

Lillian had fully accepted that Alexander was a "night" person, and he would rest during the day. Although she accepted the fact, she also knew that as a very successful businessman with large estates to oversee, there was much more going on with him than she was aware. And it piqued her interest.

So, she used her days to read everything that she could to confirm the suspicions she had about her love, but in the end, she realized that it didn't really matter to her why he was unavailable during the day. Nothing mattered to her as long as they could be together.

It became the pattern for Lillian and Alexander to spend every evening together. He would hold her while she read to him and then sing her to sleep.

He always came bearing gifts. The things he called trinkets were actually beautiful, old, and unique pieces of jewelry and museum-quality antiques. The shelves of her hidden personal library were now graced with one-of-a-kind first edition books and wonderful perfumes. Oils from faraway lands sat upon her dressing table.

One month turned into four and the melodies with which Alexander calmed her fears each night haunted her subconscious, even during the day.

During this time, when they were outside, the shadowy figures that seem to be just out of Lillian's range of sight continued to follow them. Alexander's apparent acceptance of their presence had calmed some of her fears, but her anxiety increased every time one of them entered into her field of vision. One night, they were out walking in the gardens and a man appeared on the pathway directly in front of them.

Lillian felt Alexander tense and then, with gentle pressure, he slowly pushed her behind him. It was obvious to her that Alexander knew the man, but he didn't speak as the intruder casually walked towards them.

As the imposing man drew closer, she realized that the gentleman was similar to Alexander in many ways. Pale skinned, tall, dark, and mesmerizingly handsome.

"It's time, Alexander. Time to take your place," the man said after stopping just a few feet away from the couple.

"I make those decisions; not you. Tell the others that I have no desire to join you at this time or any other."

"There will be consequences; you realize that, of course."

"There always are."

The man turned and, with a one last glance back at them, appeared to blur and then disappeared into the night.

Alexander sighed and then turned to Lillian.

"I need to get you home."

She pulled him close and kissed him deeply. "There is nothing that you can't tell me, my love, nothing."

CHAPTER TWO

Two days passed and, on the evening of the third day, with no word from Alexander, Lillian finally decided to take the situation into her own hands. Women her age never went out alone, but after declining an invitation to join the rest of her family at the palace for a formal reception, she sneaked down to the stables and demanded a carriage. After swearing the stable boys to secrecy, she instructed the driver to take her to Alexander's estate.

It took almost an hour for the imposing silhouette of the massive manor house to appear in the distance. Soon, her coach rolled up to the imposing entryway.

"Wait for me here. If I don't come out after an hour, you may go back home."

"But, miss, your father will have my head if I leave you here alone. Please, I beg you, get back into the carriage and let me take you home."

"Do as I tell you!" she instructed sternly, knowing that if she didn't demand the respect of her station, the driver would, through fear, disregard all of her instruction and would act on his own "for her own protection." Lillian turned and, lifting her heavy skirts, walked determinedly up the many stairs leading to the formal entrance of Alexander's mansion.

She used the large brass knocker and heard the echo down the hall as the pounding announced her presence.

When no servant came to the door, she tried the handle and, much to her surprise, the heavy door opened without hesitation.

"Alexander?" she called into the darkness of the entranceway.

The house was completely dark, but Lillian was compelled to enter. Finding a lamp and matches on the console just inside the door to her right, she quickly lit the lamp. In the yellow glow of its light, she stood quietly, letting her instincts tell her which way to go.

"I should be frightened," she thought, "But I'm not. If Alex is here, I'm going to find him."

"Alexander? It's Lillian. I need to see you," she called as she continued to walk.

"You shouldn't have come, Lillian," she heard from behind her.

She turned to find an Alexander she'd never seen before. His eyes glowed red, giving him a menacing look. She also noticed the lengthened canines that confirmed her research. Alexander was indeed a vampire. She had suspected as much for quite some time now.

"I love you, Alex, and I'll not let anything keep us apart."

"I don't frighten you?"

Alexander seemed shocked by her response to his true self and instantly changed back to his usual form.

"I'm not the naive girl you believed me to be, Alex," she said, stepping closer while reaching up to stroke his handsome face.

Alex kissed her, lifting her off the floor and into his arms.

"Let me join you," she begged. "I wish never to be parted from you."

Instantly serious, Alexander considered her request for a moment before responding, "Your family will be lost to you; this life is not the life of romantic notions you think it is. I'm a killer, Lillian. I must kill to exist. And although I can walk amongst your kind in the light of day, it leaves me vulnerable and weak."

"I don't care. I have read all the books available to me on the subject of your condition, and I make this request of you regardless. You, my love, are worth any of the consequences that were described. You must grant my wish."

Alex kissed her again.

"Take the carriage home; I will come to you after midnight."

"My door remains unlocked. My family won't miss me, Alex."

"I will see that they receive a sum equal to the dowry that would be granted to the family of your intended, should you have been engaged to marry. It will be a sum befitting your station. I expect that your family will be mollified by the double bonus of that money. But, Lillian, you will never see your family again."

"They don't see me now, Alex. Even when I'm in the same room, I am invisible to them. Before I met you, I was already making plans to leave my family and to make my own way in the world. Toward that end, my father signed what he thought were permissions for me to study art in France. Unbeknownst to him, what he really signed were authorizations for monies to be transferred to accounts in Switzerland in my own name. This money would free me and enable me to do as I wish."

Alexander smiled as they approached the front hall and he set Lillian down.

"I feel sorry for your family, my love. Their loss will be so much more than they will ever know. You are the most amazing woman, Lillian. That they don't know that, leads me to think ill of them. They don't deserve you; therefore, I have no regrets."

He kissed her again and then opened the door and watched as she descended the stairs, and entered the waiting coach. He stood at the door watching, until the coach disappeared into the now fog-filled night.

Lillian arrived at her home well before her family's expected return from dinner. These affairs always seemed to last late into the evening.

Knowing that this would be the last night she spent in her parents' home, she took time to wander through the rooms she loved most: the library, the front parlors, and the gallery.

Returning to her room, she packed the few precious objects that she wished to take with her and waited impatiently for Alexander.

Finally, exhaustion won and she curled up on her side and drifted off to sleep.

"I'm here my love," she heard Alexander whisper, but did not wake. "You will be my bride, not only in this time, but for eternity. We will forever be joined once your life's blood is transferred to me and then back to you. While the pain you feel will be fleeting, our love for one another will not."

What happened next was as if in a dream. He lifted her to him, letting her head fall naturally away from him, exposing her delicate neck.

He took in her scent before baring his elongated canines and piercing the throbbing vein on her throat.

Lillian winced and drew a sharp breath. Surprisingly, the assault of pain was tempered by a growing surge of pleasure that turned the scream she had barely held back into the moan that now escaped her open lips.

In mere moments, Alexander felt her essence fading away. It took all of his strength to then stop his feeding and the chance that he would actually end her life before it began.

She looked so beautiful. He had never wanted any woman more. Alexander lowered Lillian's near lifeless body to the bed and knelt beside it. He pulled the sleeve back on his right arm, exposing his wrist, before using his teeth to open the vein now pulsing with Lillian's blood. He held his arm up, over her head, letting the blood drip into her mouth.

It took only seconds for Lillian's nostrils to flare. She looked up at him and they shared a moment in time confirming their bond before her wild need took over and she grabbed his arm, feeding as a vampire for the very first time.

Now it was Alexander who felt pain mixed an intense pleasure. He would never willingly leave her, he knew that now.

He carried her to his waiting carriage and then into his house and up into his bed.

"How do you feel, my love?"

"I grow stronger by the second. Make love to me now, Alex. Let us truly be one."

They consummated the joining of their blood and their love for one another. Lillian was no longer a human or a virgin.

"You will sleep now until the hunger comes. I must hunt, but I won't be far away."

That was the last time she heard Alexander's voice or was able to look upon this face.

Lillian awoke now in unfamiliar surroundings, hearing loud voices coming from the hallway.

Everything told Lillian that she had to run, to get away, seek out a hiding place, and give Alex time to find her. But she was too weak to act upon her instinct.

The door squealed open. Lillian pretended to be asleep. She felt apprehensive as the two males entering the room approached her.

A gruff voice announced, "I know you can hear me. Your lover is dead to you. You will stay with us until we tire of you."

"You're a cruel one," the other voice responded. "She is beautiful. Do you plan to keep her in a dormant state the whole time?"

"She'll be less trouble that way. We'll feed her just enough to keep her alive. It's Alex we are interested in, not her, although she might be a nice diversion."

They left, but Lillian noticed that she didn't hear them lock the door.

Where am I? What's happened? she thought as she strained to open her eyes. She was very determined to get away, but how? Was Alex really dead?

She had studied vampires and vampire lore for weeks before Alex himself had confirmed her suspicions. Their kind could walk in the light, but it made their powers much weaker. It was of course true they needed blood to survive and this was confirmed by the craving that she was experiencing now. This hunger was painful and all consuming.

Something truly must have happened to Alex. Lillian knew he would never have left her otherwise. From her investigations of vampire lore, she knew that without fresh blood, her body would try to preserve her life and shut down until only the barest vestige of "life" was in her. She also knew that she only had a very narrow window in which to act. She would go dormant again very soon. From the way that she felt, she must have been fed recently, but not enough to push back the craving. Then she heard something rustling in the room with her. Her now enhanced senses told her that whatever it was, it had warm blood coursing through its veins. It was her sense of smell that told her it was a rat.

Obtaining the prey would take every ounce of strength that she had. She would be taking a chance using too much of her energy reserves, but she knew she had to try.

Lillian drew a deep breath and held it for a moment. She knew she would only have only this one chance. She concentrated on the rat's location. The sound of the rat getting closer was deafeningly loud to her new vampire hearing.

"Come closer," she silently begged.

It was now or never. The speed she now possessed surprised her. She dropped so quickly on the rat it never knew what hit it. She plunged her virgin fangs deep into its flesh and, as she drained it dry, she could feel its life's blood rejuvenating her body and her spirit.

Lillian knew that the strength afforded by one rat wasn't enough to get her to full strength, of course, but hoped that it would be enough to get her away from whoever was holding her.

She was being held in a small, dark, windowless cube. The small bed was its only piece of furniture. Lillian had heard the door squeal when opened and deduced that the door was metal. That squeal was going to be an obstacle to her freedom.

Her senses were stronger now that she'd fed, so she sniffed the air for any trace of another being and found none. Her captors were most likely hunting. Thinking that she was dormant, and would be for some time, they had left her alone.

Lillian crept to the door and pushed it open a crack, peering out into the darkness that was now illuminated by her new vampire vision.

She pushed hard against the door and opened it just enough to squeeze through. Once again, she sniffed the air, this time looking for a way out.

Sensing fresh air from her right, she shifted that way. Her body moved like lightning. She had no idea how long the strength from small amount of blood newly flowing in her veins would last, but only that she had to get as far away as fast as she possibly could.

Three days later, she was on a ship heading to America. The funds she had diverted to accounts in her name were her saving grace now.

As Lillian stood on the moonlight drenched deck, she pulled a letter out of her pocket and re-read it one more time.

"You are dead to us; never contact us again."

She had shamed her parents when she ran away to be with Alex, and although she had hoped otherwise, she had expected a response like this when she sent them her message.

She crumbled up the short letter and tossed it over the railing into the cold, dark Atlantic waters and knew that from this point on, she was her own and her life had begun anew.

I'm going to live for me now, not for anyone else, Lillian thought. *Strange, they told me Alex was dead, but for some reason, I don't feel that. Alex told me we would always be connected by the blood we shared. No, he is alive. If I can feel him, he can feel me. He'll find me, I'm sure of it.*

"I need to feed," she said softly under her breath.

Lillian found her new power over humans quite seductive and she rather enjoyed it.

She walked along the ship's railing and, before long, saw a deckhand scrubbing down the promenade just ahead.

Lillian picked up her skirts as she walked by, intentionally showing him a tantalizing bit of her ankle.

He took in the view and then looked up at her face. Lillian smiled and deepened her gaze. She offered her hand and he stood, completely mesmerized by her.

He wasn't much older than her, and she knew his blood would taste ever so sweet.

She drew him close and licked the nape of his neck, causing him to moan. She punctured the skin just beneath his collar and quickly fed. When she finished, the young man's knees were a little weak, more from the pleasure than the taking of blood.

"You better finish your work. I hope to see you again sometime," Lillian said as she backed away.

The young man just nodded and returned to his duties as if nothing had happened.

Slowly sauntering away, Lillian smiled smugly to herself.

She entered her quarters, proud of the fact that they were the best and the largest available on ship. Money was not ever going to be a problem for her. She had spent a year siphoning money away from many of her family's accounts. She was so clever and deft that no one ever even suspected a thing.

Her family had been wrong to underestimate and dismiss her. Alex was right; they didn't deserve to be a part of her life.

CHAPTER THREE

In the past Lillian would have been able to summon up remorse at the thought of leaving her family. But that emotion evaporated the night she met Alex. And now, even without him, somehow she knew as she always had that she would be all right on her own. In fact, were he here, Alex would be proud of her.

"If you don't find me, Alex, I am going to find you."

~~~~

After World War I, Lillian stopped thinking about Alex every day. By World War II, he was a distant memory, an old scar; healed, but still there.

She had made a success of herself in America. She was wealthy, well known, and a much sought after photographer of celebrities, a publisher, and filmmaker. She was undoubtedly one of the first females to get to the top in each of her chosen endeavors. She loved the power business afforded her. In her love life, though, she always kept things casual and brief.

"Most vampires stay in the shadows, yet you flourish out in the open. How do you do it, Lillian?" Ashton asked, appearing next to her as she walked the dark pathways of the Hollywood hills.

"We aren't the vampires of the movies, are we, Ashton?" Lillian said without slowing her stride.

"But you continue to look so young. Don't they ask you about it?"

"I tell them my agelessness is because of "my beauty regimen." And I do plan to put out a skin care line. I also tell them to stay out of the sun, like I do. I haven't seen you in quite some time, Ashton. What have you been up to?"

"You asked me once to find you if I had any information on the Lexerus."

Lillian stopped. "You have my attention; go on."

"They meet," he whispered. "It is said that the leadership will be challenged."

Lillian's eyes narrowed. "Why now? What else have you heard, Ashton?"

"Humans are at war again, as you know. It's creating a feeding frenzy in Europe. Many have been turned and, through sloppiness, for the first time in centuries, our numbers are rising. The council fears that we on the path that could lead to our discovery, that our existence will be revealed. Not all vampires are as discrete as we are, Lillian."

"Maybe it's time we had our own representation on the Council, or an American Council of our own."

"You really think the Lexerus would allow that? Forget this idea, Lillian."

"You're right, Ashton. The time is not right. Will you keep me informed? I want to know what the Lexerus decides."

"You know I will."

They walked in silence for a few yards before Ashton spoke.

"Lillian, I helped you forget about your lost love once. I don't suppose you would let me stay with you for a while?"

"I'm a loner, Ashton. You know that."

"Making money and running a business is not living, Lillian. You need others. If not me, let someone else in."

Lillian started to walk again. "I love my life. I do what I want, when I want. Thank you for your concern, Ashton, but I like things just the way they are."

"You put on a good act, I must say. Be careful that you don't actually start to believe it. Good bye, Lillian."

All that remained of him was a hint of his scent in the air.

Using equal vampire speed, Lillian now hunted. She found prey. A man just returning home from some late night rendezvous, she supposed. Liquor assailed her nostrils as she stopped inches from him.

Before another breath entered his lungs, her fangs drew life-giving blood from the side of his neck, causing his knees to weaken. She felt first his fear, and then his euphoria as part of his life passed to her.

"You will sleep peacefully," she whispered. She licked the punctures, healing them instantly and left him leaning against his door.

She watched from afar as he fought off his lethargy, then, standing erect, flexing his shoulders several times, he finally pulled at his jacket and shook his head before entering the house.

She marveled at the ease of it and wondered to herself that others of her kind would actually resort to taking life in order to feed themselves.

The next day, Lillian sat in her office looking out the window, deep in thought. Photos she'd taken of her friends, some of the most famous people of the day, covered her walls and were listed in her phone directory. Emerging from her contemplation, she realized that Ashton was right; it wasn't enough to just be successful in business.

Lillian buzzed her secretary, "Victoria, get Marcus on the phone for me, will you please?"

In a few minutes, Victoria buzzed back, "Marcus is on the line."

"Marcus, I want you to sell all my business interests. I have something I need to do and I can't be tied down here. I know it's sudden. Just do it. And Marcus, I expect the best price; you understand me, don't you? Good; I'll be in touch."

Lillian changed her name like humans changed vehicles. Money could buy you anything you needed and ingenuity took care of the rest. She was smart, tough, and trusted her instincts. Although she favored her own name, for her personal security she could only use that persona once every quarter century. This time, she chose Valerie; Valerie Windsor.

It took months to set up all the new accounts, background information, and corporations before she was ready to go into a new business and start again. This time around, she established a holding company and a set of corporations centered on hotels; another male-dominated venture. That was the challenge and the fun; pitting herself against the most successful men in an industry. She built this new business from the ground up, literally. Continually prospecting for, buying, and then renovating historic properties. Soon, every major city on the East Coast had added a hotel to her dynasty.

After twenty very successful years of the marshalling one of the largest, most profitable, and widely desirable, privately held hotel empires, it was not enough. Valerie was well known for surrounding herself with the smartest, best trained, and most innovative persons, paying them what they were worth, and letting them do their jobs. Her large group of employees were fiercely loyal to the man. The corporations were running smoothly now and Valerie found that she was once again bored.

~~~~~

It was now nineteen seventy-eight and she was going home.

"Now don't worry about anything here," Ronnie, her assistant said. "You've built an amazing group just for this reason. We'll take care of everything."

"I am so grateful that we found each other, Ronnie. I know you will watch over everything for me."

"Well, you really saved me, Valerie. If I, as a new vampire, would have been left alone, I never would have lasted. You are my dearest friend." After a short pause, Ronnie asked, "You're going to the meeting of the Lexerus, aren't you?"

"I'm thinking about it. Maybe, maybe not. I'll seek out some vampires and get a feeling for the circumstances surrounding this gathering. Usually, there is a specific reason for a meeting, but this time, no one seems to know why it has been called."

The next evening, she snuggled into her first class seat on the airplane and thought back on her life. She had done what she'd set out to do. To her immense satisfaction, she'd done it all on her own.

A man set his briefcase down on the seat next to her and handed his carry-on luggage to the attendant.

He smelled delicious.

"Hello," he said with a sexy smile.

"Would you like some champagne, Mister Alistair?" the stewardess asked.

"That would be fine."

"And you, Miss Windsor?"

"Tequila with lime, please."

This request raised Alistair's eyebrow.

"Business or pleasure?" he asked.

"Excuse me?"

"Your trip to England. Business or pleasure?"

"Business," she said coolly.

"Here you are, champagne for you and tequila with lime for you."

"Thank you," they both told the stewardess.

"I'm going home," Alistair said, raising his glass in salute.

"Me too," Valerie said under her breath.

"I'm sorry, did you say something?"

"My family is from London. Well, my ancestors. I may try to look up some relatives while I'm there."

"I'm from London, born and raised there. Maybe I could help."

"I could tell from your accent. Thank you, but I'm not even sure if I'll have time."

"Let me introduce myself. I'm Chase Alistair," he said, extending his hand.

"Valerie Windsor," she replied, looking him deep in the eyes.

Chase's expression never changed; he was strong personality and very handsome man, in a mysterious way.

She shook his hand and smiled back at him.

"This sounds like such a line, but have we met before?"

"It does sound like a line, but no, I don't think so. I would hope you would have remembered more clearly if we had."

"Sorry, your name is not familiar, but your face, your voice..." he said, seemingly desperate to recall the memory.

"I would certainly have remembered you," she said, breaking his concentration.

"Nice of you to say so. Windsor, is that the family you are searching for, because I think I know where you can find some," he said with an ironic chuckle.

"No, Whillenhaul, actually. A much more interesting side of the family."

"What else are you looking for in England?"

"A...a hotel, or a manor house that I can turn into a hotel."

"Good luck, not that you will need it. I buy and sell companies. I've been doing it for twenty-five years, since I dropped out of college. The States offered the opportunities for the best return on my investment, so that's where I had to be. Now, I guess I just don't have the passion for it anymore. So I sold everything and I'm going home."

"No Mrs. Alistair?"

"I never made the time. Commitment wasn't on my agenda. I was too busy building my company. Not that I didn't have chances. And children? Definitely not for me; I knew I was too selfish. You?"

"I have to say that your story sounds very familiar. In fact, it could have come from my mouth. Do you regret that now?"

"I don't regret things; it's a waste of time. After all, I'm not dead yet. I have plenty of time to do anything I want. In fact, I don't have to work anymore at all, if I don't want to." He paused. "I sound like I'm trying to convince myself, don't I?"

"Again, the story sounds all too familiar. I have plenty of time too, a lifetime."

"We seem to have a lot in common. Sure you won't change your mind about getting together?"

"Perhaps."

This wasn't like her, she thought. She felt like a giddy school girl. She was, after all ,one hundred and eight years old.

Valerie had planned to sleep on the way over, but she and Chase had such interesting conversations on numerous topics and the time quickly passed. She hadn't felt like this since…since her time with Alex. And a human man?

The announcement came to fasten their seatbelts. They would be landing in just a few minutes.

"I usually detest these long flights and try to sleep through them. Today, I find myself wishing it was just a bit longer," Chase said as they gathered up their things.

"Are you staying with family?"

"No," Chase said. "I said I was coming home. I meant to London. My family and I don't exactly get along. Actually, I never felt a part of my family for some reason. They call it a 'bad family dynamic.' Anyway, too much drama for me. No, I purchased an estate twenty minutes outside London. How about you, Valerie?"

"I rented one."

"Really, where?

"In Surrey," Valerie said as she prepared to leave.

"We might as well share a car then, because that is where my estate is."

"You're just saying that. I mean, what are the odds?"

"Today, I would say they are pretty good."

Valerie smiled and shook her head. It was all so strange, but somehow, it felt right. To Chase, she said, "I have arranged for my own transportation, and I do have some stops to make before I go to my rental."

Chase looked genuinely disappointed. "I will be going then. I should have a car waiting for me. If we are neighbors, I'm sure we'll be seeing more of each other."

They exited the plane and walked towards the transportation area.

"How about tomorrow?"

"You are persistent. Tomorrow, I am going to look at property."

"Well, you have to eat, don't you?"

Actually, she didn't. Vampires could eat food, but didn't need to. "How about Friday? We both need some time to get settled, right?"

"Miss Windsor?" a driver asked.

"Yes, get my bags, will you please?" She smiled at Chase. "Here's my address; is eight o'clock all right?"

"Yes. I guess I'll try to find a decorator tomorrow then. I am sure the house will need a lot of work."

"Those are just the kind I like."

"I'm sure you have excellent taste."

"Yes, I do. Goodbye, Chase."

Books by Elizabeth Loraine:

Royal Blood Chronicles Series

- *Katrina - the Beginning*

- *The Protectors*

- *The Dark Prince*

- *Cain – the Quest*

- *Bloodline*

- *Legacy*

- *Redemption*

- *Destiny*

- *Royal Chronicles Short Stories*

- *Quinn – a Watchers Story*

- *Marcella – Vampire Mage*

Phantom Lives Series

- *Collier*
- *Power*

Other Books

- *Lillian – A Vampire Tale*
- *Lillian – Mask*
- *Green River – Shifter Chronicle*
- *Corporate Ties- a Silken Series* – Adult Contemporary

~~~BIBLIOGRAPHY~~~

Andom, M. (2007). A course explores the cultural manifestations of vampires. Chronicles of Higher Education, 54 (11), 10.

Ball, A. (Director). (2008). True blood [Television Series]. Baton Rouge.

Barnett, R. (2009, March 9). Why do we love vampires. Retrieved April 10, 2009, from ivillage: htto://www.ivillage.com

Bartlett, W. &. (2005). Legends of blood: the vampire in history and myth. Glouchester: Sutton Publishing.

Blasingame, J. (2006). Books for adolescents. Journal of Adolescent and Adult Literacy, 49 (7), 628-633.

Blue, D. M. (2011). The Annotated Carmilla.

Blue, D. M (2012) Striking a Chord (A Look at Harry Potter, Twilight, and The Hunger Games)

Cheung, T. (2009). The Element Encyclopedia of Vampires. Metra Books.

Coppola, F. F. (Director). (1992). Bram Stoker's Dracula [Motion Picture].

Cutoni, V. (1993, June). The discreet charm of the vampire. Urania, p. 27.

Day, W. P. (2002). Vampire legends in contemporary American culture: What becomes a legend most. Lexington: University of Kentucky Press.

Deich, D. V. (2011, March). (B. Varney, Interviewer)

DeLaCruz, M. (2007). Blue bloods. New York: Hyperion Books.

DeMarco, J. (1997). Vampire literature: Something young adults can really sink their teeth into. Emergency Librarian , 24 (5), 26.

Dixon-Kennedy, M. (1998). Encyclopedia of Greco-Roman Mythology,. Santa Barbara: ABC-Clio.

Dukes, P. (1982). Dracula: Fact, legend and fiction. History Today , 32 (7), 44.

England, T. V. (2011, April). (B. Varney, Interviewer)

Florida vs. Rod Ferrell : The vampire cult slaying case. (2001, June 22). Retrieved February 25, 2009, from Court TV: http://www.courttv.com/archive/verdicts/vampire.html

Frakes, J. (Director). (2008). The Librarian: The curse of the Judas chalice [Motion Picture].

Gresh, L. (2008). The Twilight companion; The unauthorized guide to the series. New York: Saint Martin's Press.

Grimal - Editor, P. (1982). Larousse World Mythology . NY: Excalibur Books.

Hamilton, J. (2007). The World of Horror, Vampire. Edina, Minn: Abdo Publishing Company.

Harper, C. and McFall, K. (2010). The Cowboy and The Vampire. Midnight Ink.

Harper, C. and McFall, K. (2012). Blood and Whiskey. Midnight Ink.

Harris, C. (2005). Dead as a doornail. New York: Ace Books: Berkley Publishing Group.

Harris, C. (2001). Dead until dark. New York: Ace Books: Berkley Publisher Group.

Harris, C. (2006). Definitely dead. New York: Ace Books: Berkley Publishing Group.

Harris, C. (2009). Q and a with Charlaine. Retrieved April 24, 2009, from Charlaine Harris: www.charlaineharris.com

Hefner, A. G. (2003, March 9). Lilith. Retrieved February 14, 2009, from The Encyclopedia Mythica: http://www.angelfire.com/realm/shades/demons/emlilith.htm

Hilburn, L. (2007). The vampire shrink. New York: Medallion Press.

Hilburn, L. (2008, October 30). Why do women love vampires. Retrieved March 9, 2009, from Paranormality Universe: www.paranormalityuniversity.blogspot.com

Holst, J. (2002). Advertising mascots. Retrieved March 29, 2009, from TV Acres: http://www.tvacres.com/admascots_chocula.htm

Hood, S. (2001). Aloft with Lilith. Performing Arts and Entertainment in Canada, 33 (3), 26.

Howe, J. &. (1979). Bunnicula the vampire bunny. New York: Scholastic, Inc.

Huff, T. (1991). Blood price. New York: Daw Books.

Humphrey, C. (2007, April). Not your mother's vampire: vampires in young adult fiction. History Today, 53 (4), p. 175.

Joslin, L. (2006). Count Dracula goes to the movies (2nd ed.). Jefferson, North Carolina: McFarland & Co.

Karg, B. S. (2009). The everything vampire book; from Vlad the Impaler to the vampire Lestat- the history of vampires in literature film and legend. Avon: Adams Media.

Koogler, Audrey (2011, March). (B. Varney, Interviewer)

Le Fanu, J. S. (1872). Carmilla. Ireland.

Leekley, J. (Director). (1996). Kindred the embraced tv series [Motion Picture].

Levin, G. (nd). Fans drink up "True Blood" Booklist.

Lilith Fair. (1999, September 15). Retrieved February 14, 2009, from Lilith Fair: http://lilithfair.com/index.html

Littleton- Editor, C. S. (2002). Mythology, The Illustrated Anthology of World Myths and Storytelling. London: Duncan Baird Publishers.

Lui, J. (2004, May). Vampire: The masquerade- bloodlines. Computer Gaming World, 4.

Lussier, P. (Director). (2000). Dracula 2000 [Motion Picture].

Lyons, R. (2007). Daystar. Macon: Samhain Publishing.

Lyons, R. (2006). Midnight sun. Macon: Samhain Publishing.

Lyons, R. (2007). Tempting darkness. Macon: Samhain Publishing.

McNally, R. T. (1994). In Search of Dracula. Houghton Mifflin.

Meloni, C. (2007). The rise of vampire literature. Library Media Connection, 26 (2), 30-33.

Melton, J. G. (1998). The Vampire gallery. Detroit: Visible Ink PRess.

Melton, J. (2010). The Vampire Book. Farminghills, MI: Visible Ink Press.

Meyer, S. (2006). New moon. New York: Little Brown and Company.

Meyer, S. (2005). Twilight. New York: Little Brown and Company.

Norrington, S. (Director). (1998). Blade [Motion Picture].

Nuzum, E. (2007). The dead travel fast: Stalking vampires from Nosferatu to Count Chocula. New York: Saint Martin's Press.

Osherow, M. (2000). The dawn of a new Lilith: Revisionary mythmaking in women's science fiction. NWSA Journal, 12 (1), 68-83.

Paul, N. (2005, October 15). Bloody good reads: Vampire tales with bite. Library Journal, p. 96.

Paulson, K. (Ed.). (2009, January). Does "Twilight" prove that vampires are real? USA Today, p. 9.

Peardon, K. (1999). Vampires in modern culture. Retrieved March 29, 2009, from Everything you need to know about vampires: http://www.angelfire.com/tn/vampires/index.html

Pecos, H. (2011, March). Creator of The Federal Vampire and Zombie Agency. (B. Varney, Interviewer)

Prest, S. (1845). Varney the vampire. London: Ayer Company Publishers.

Ramsland, K. (1989, November). Hunger for the marvelous: The vampire craze in the computer age. Psychology Today, 37-42.

Ransim, A. (2007, May 7). Judas Iscariot: the first vampire. Retrieved February 25, 2009, from Darkness Embraced: www.darknessembraced.com

Rappaport, A. (1989). Ancient Israel myths and legends. New York: Bonanza Books.

Rein-Hagn, M. (1991). Vampire the masquerade. Iceland: White Wolf.

Scarvone, D. (1990). Vampires: Opposing viewpoints. Farming Hills: Greenhaven Press.

Schreiber, E. (2003). Vampire kisses. New York: HarperTeen.

Schumaker, J. (Director). (1987). The Lost Boys [Motion Picture].

Seltzer, S. (2008, November 26). That's what vampires are for: Fangs, sex and society. Retrieved February 4, 2009, from Huffington Post: www.huffingtonpost.com/sarah-seltzer

Stevenson, S. (2002). The complete idiot's guide to vampires. Indianapolis: Alpha Books.

Stoker, B. (1897). Dracula. London: Archibald Constable and Company.

Storm, H. (Director). (1985). Once Bitten [Motion Picture].

The King James Version of The Holy Bible.

Williams, E. R. (2006). Adolescent television viewing and belief in vampires. Journal of Belief and Values, 27 (2), 227-229.

www.ingramcontent.com/pod-product-compliance
Lightning Source LLC
Chambersburg PA
CBHW060242290526
45789CB00001B/163